MW01103454

The Complete IDIOT'S Guide to WORDPERFECT® FOR WINDOWS™

by Paul McFedries

alpha books

A Division of Prentice Hall Computer Publishing
201 W. 103rd Street, Indianapolis, Indiana 46290 USA

To Karen: For those times when you need to give WordPerfect technical support to total strangers in Thai restaurants.

©1993 Alpha Books

International Standard Book Number: 1-56761-282-2
Library of Congress Catalog Card Number: 93-71736

96 95 94 93   8 7 6 5 4 3 2 1

Interpretation of the printing code: the rightmost number of the first series of numbers is the year of the book's printing; the rightmost number of the second series of numbers is the number of the book's printing. For example, a printing code of 93-1 shows that the first printing of the book occurred in 1993.

Screen reproductions in this book were created by means of the program Collage Plus from Inner Media, Inc., Hollis, NH.

Printed in the United States of America

The Complete Idiot's WordPerfect for Windows Reference Card

WordPerfect's Wondrous Windows

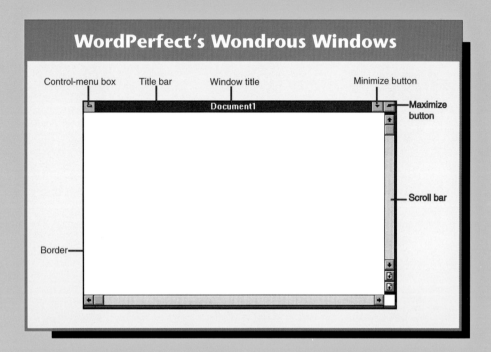

Cool Tip #1

Mouse users get an extra bonus in version 6: QuickMenus. These menus display a short list of commands related to a specific feature. All you do is place the mouse pointer over the feature (such as the typing area) and then right-click. When the menu appears, just click (left button this time) on the command you want.

Cool Tip #2

Use "drag-and-drop" to move text in the blink of an eye. Just select the text (by dragging over it with your mouse), put the mouse pointer inside the block, hold down the left mouse button, drag the text to the new location, and then release the button.

Mouse Movements

Point   Move the mouse pointer so it rests on a specific screen location.

Click   Quickly press and release the left mouse button.

Double-click   Quickly press and release the left mouse button twice in succession.

Drag   Press and hold down the left mouse button.

alpha books

Caveat Dept.

Computers, being the temperamental beasts that they are, often seem to be just accidents waiting for a place to happen. Here are a few tips to help keep you out of trouble:

- ☞ If you ever find yourself on some strange WordPerfect for Windows turf and you're starting to feel nervous about what may happen next, press **Esc** until you're back on more familiar ground. Esc is an all-purpose bailout key that should get you out of most sticky-wickets unscathed.

- ☞ Never shut off your computer while WordPerfect for Windows is still running. Doing so can lead to lost data, trashed files, and unsightly warts.

- ☞ You should save your work (by selecting the **S**ave command from the File menu, or by pressing **Ctrl+S**) as often as you possibly can. You never know when a power outage or program crash may strike and blow away an afternoon's work.

- ☞ If you're trying to navigate with the numeric keypad, but all you get are numbers, press the **Num Lock** key.

- ☞ Only move or rename files that you've created yourself. Monkeying with any other files could cause WordPerfect to go on strike for better working conditions.

- ☞ Unless you have special "undelete" software, any files you delete are gone for good, so you should be absolutely sure you can live without a file before getting rid of it.

- ☞ Speller and Grammatik are useful tools, but they're no substitute for either a flesh-and-blood dictionary or a thorough proofreading. Don't be lazy!

- ☞ Back up your documents regularly. If you don't have backup software, you can use File Manager's Copy command to back up your files to a floppy disk. There are *no* excuses!

The Power Bar: Easy Everyday Access

WordPerfect for Windows version 6 includes a fancy new Power Bar tool that puts common tasks only a mouse click away. The hard part is figuring out what those tiny little pictures mean! To help, here's a rundown of each tool:

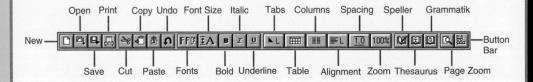

Cool Tip #3

If you have a favorite spot in a document, you can label it with a special bookmark called a QuickMark. Just position the insertion point on the spot and press **Ctrl+Shift+Q**. To find the QuickMark, just press **Ctrl+Q**. Now *that's* quick!

Cool Tip #4

The default Button Bar gives you access to a dozen of WordPerfect for Windows' most common commands. But don't forget: there are 11 other Button Bars designed for specific tasks. To see a list, right-click on the Button Bar.

Publisher
Marie Butler-Knight

Associate Publisher
Lisa A. Bucki

Managing Editor
Elizabeth Keaffaber

Acquisitions Manager
Stephen R. Poland

Development Editor
Faithe Wempen

Production Editor
Linda Hawkins

Manuscript Editor
Audra Gable

Cover Designer
Scott Cook

Designer
Roger Morgan

Indexer
Craig A.Small

Production Team
*Gary Adair, Diana Bigham, Katy Bodenmiller,
Brad Chinn, Tim Cox, Meshell Dinn, Mark Enochs,
Howard Jones, Beth Rago, Carrie Roth, Greg Simsic, Marc Shecter*

*Special thanks to C. Herbert Feltner for ensuring the
technical accuracy of this book.*

Contents at a Glance

Contents

Introduction

If you've ever tried to have a conversation with a so-called computer "expert," then you know they have this uncanny ability to make the rest of us feel like complete idiots within five seconds. They prattle on in their techno-jargon, throwing in the odd "of course" and "obviously" to make it clear that any fool with half a brain ought to know this stuff. Nuts to them, I say! Not only are we *not* idiots, but we're smart enough to know a thing or two ourselves:

- ☞ We're smart enough to know that "cool" isn't defined by how many back issues of *Popular Mechanics* we keep in the bathroom. We simply don't need a lot of technical details (and we don't wear pocket protectors, either).

- ☞ We're smart enough to know that it doesn't make sense to learn absolutely *everything* about WordPerfect. We just need to know enough to get our work done, thank you.

- ☞ We're smart enough to know that life's too short to read five kazillion pages of arcane (and mostly useless) information. We have lives to lead, after all.

A Book for Smart WordPerfect Idiots

If you're no fool, but the computer gurus of the world make you feel like one, then welcome to *The Complete Idiot's Guide to WordPerfect for Windows*! This is a book for those of us who aren't (and don't even want to be) computer wizards. This is a book for those of us who have a job to do—a job that includes working with WordPerfect—and we just want to get it done as quickly and painlessly as possible. This *isn't* one of those absurdly serious, put-a-crease-in-your-brow-and-we'll-begin kinds of books. On the contrary, we'll even try to have—gasp!—a little fun as we go along.

You'll also be happy to know that this book doesn't assume you have any previous experience with WordPerfect. This means that we'll begin each topic at the beginning, and build your knowledge from there. But you won't find any long-winded discussions of boring technical details. With *The Complete Idiot's Guide to WordPerfect for Windows*, you get just the facts you *need* to know, not everything there *is* to know. All the information is presented in short, easy-to-digest chunks that you can easily skim through to find just the information you want.

How This Book Is Set Up

I'm assuming you have a life away from your computer screen, so *The Complete Idiot's Guide to WordPerfect for Windows* is set up so that you don't have to read it cover to cover. If you want to know how to print, for example, just turn to the printing chapter. To make things easier to find, I've organized the book into five more or less sensible sections:

Part I—Day-to-Day Skills

WordPerfect follows the old 80-20 rule: you'll spend 80 percent of your time working with 20 percent of the program's features. The eight chapters in this section cover most of that 20 percent. You'll learn basic stuff, such as starting WordPerfect (Chapter 3), using the keyboard and mouse (Chapter 4), and saving your work (Chapter 7).

Part II—Getting It Right: Editing Stuff

The benefits of a word processor over a typewriter are legion, but one of the biggest is being able to edit a document right on the screen. These three chapters show you how to delete—and undelete—text (Chapter 9), how to move chunks of text around (Chapter 10), and how to find stuff in your documents (Chapter 11).

Part III—Looking Good: Formatting Stuff

Because looking good is often as important as *being* good, WordPerfect for Windows gives you a fistful of ways to format your documents. The four chapters in Part III introduce you to these various options. You'll learn how to format individual characters (Chapter 12), lines and paragraphs (Chapter 13), pages (Chapter 14), and more.

Part IV—Working with Documents

The stuff you create in WordPerfect—your letters, memos, and mystery novels—are called *documents*. This section shows you how to print them (Chapter 16) and work with them on screen (Chapter 17). Chapter 18 tells you about some ways to move, copy, and otherwise get a grip on your files through WordPerfect for Windows.

Part V—WordPerfect for Windows Tools

The book ends with five chapters that take you through some of WordPerfect's collection of tools and utilities. Chapter 19 scopes out a few tools that'll make your life easier. Chapters 20 and 21 check out the spell checker, thesaurus, and grammar-checker that are built right into WordPerfect. And chapters 22 and 23 deal with graphics and drawing.

The Complete Idiot's Guide to WordPerfect for Windows also includes a glossary that'll help you make sense of all those bizarre computer terms, as well as a handy tear-out reference card that gives you easy access to important (or just plain cool) WordPerfect stuff.

Features of This Book

The Complete Idiot's Guide to WordPerfect for Windows is designed so you can get the information you need fast and then get on with your life. If you ever need to type something (it comes up occasionally with word processors), it will appear like this:

type this

Also, look for the following icons, which will help you learn just what you need to know:

By the Way . . .

These boxes contain notes about WordPerfect facts that are (hopefully!) interesting and useful.

This icon defines geeky computer terms in plain English.

This icon gives you technical information you can use to impress your friends (and then forget five minutes later).

This icon provides easier ways to do things on a computer, and the tips under this icon will tell you about them.

There are always dangerous ways to do things on a computer—and this icon will tell you how to avoid them.

WordPerfect made a lot of changes in the leap from version 5.2 to 6. Where there are differences, this icon points out the appropriate 5.2 instructions.

As if all this wasn't enough, you'll also get "Put It to Work" sections, which give you real-life, hands-on, practical WordPerfect projects that you can try yourself. And to make sure you're paying attention (at least a little), you'll come across the odd "What's Wrong with This Picture" section, which will give you totally unserious quizzes about what you've learned.

Acknowledgments (The Kudos and Huzzahs Dept.)

Ah, so many people to thank, so little time. Let's start with Acquisitions Editor Steve Poland: thanks for thinking of me. Development Editor Faithe Wempen: it was great being a team again; thanks for another job well done. Managing Editor Liz Keaffaber: thanks for keeping me in line (take a vacation!). Production Editor Linda Hawkins: always a pleasure. Copy Editor Audra Gable and Tech Editor Herb Feltner: thanks for making me look good.

This page unintentionally left blank.

Part I
Day-to-Day Skills

Let's face it, WordPerfect for Windows is one intimidating program: all those installation disks and the overstuffed manuals bursting at the seams. The good news is that most of that stuff doesn't apply to the likes of you and me. All we really need are a few basic features that'll let us get our work done with a minimum of fuss and bother. In a sense, that's what this whole book is about, but the chapters here in Part I set the stage for everything else. You'll be learning basic stuff such as how to start WordPerfect, how to use your keyboard and mouse, and how to use things like the pull-down menus and dialog boxes to make your life easier. Believe me, if you can get through this stuff (and if you can dress yourself, you can handle any of this), the rest will be a day at the beach.

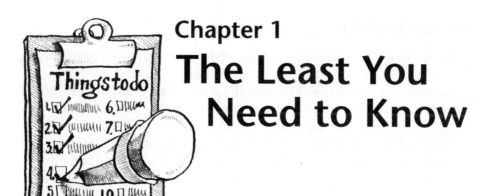

Chapter 1
The Least You Need to Know

I know, I know. You can't wait to get started. What is it? A looming dead-line? Unfettered curiosity? A type-A personality? Well, not to worry. This chapter gets you up to speed quickly by presenting a just-the-facts descrip-tion of the 10 most important WordPerfect for Windows tasks. Of course, I discuss each of these items in more detail elsewhere in the book, so if you'd like to know more, I'll also point out the relevant chapters. If you're one of those people who likes to read ahead to the good bits, this chapter's for you.

1. Entering Text

Once WordPerfect for Windows is loaded, you can start typing right away. There are no complicated commands to run, and no messy formulas to remember. You don't even have to press Enter at the end of every line, the way you do with a typewriter (where the same key is called "Return"). WordPerfect for Windows wraps your prose onto the next line, free of charge. The only time you need to press Enter is when you want to start a new paragraph. If you make a mistake, just press the Backspace key to wipe it out.

Chapter 3, "Diving In: Your First WordPerfect for Windows Session," gives you a few more tips about entering text. For the lowdown on editing your documents, skim through Part II, "Getting It Right: Editing Stuff."

2. Using Pull-Down Menus

Pull-down menus are hidden menus that list the various commands that are available for each WordPerfect for Windows task. The *menu bar* (the horizontal strip just below the top of the screen) lists the various menu names (File, Edit, View, etc.). To pull down a menu with a mouse, move the mouse pointer into the menu bar and then click on the menu name. ("Click" means to press and release the left mouse button.) From the keyboard, first find the underlined letter in the menu name. Then hold down the **Alt** key and press that letter.

Once your menu is displayed, you select a command. With a mouse, you simply click on the command. With your keyboard, you use the up and down arrow keys to highlight the command you want and then press **Enter**.

To learn more about pull-down menus, see Chapter 5, "Using WordPerfect for Windows' Pull-Down Menus."

3. Opening a Document

When you start WordPerfect for Windows, you get a blank screen that's ready for your input. If you'd prefer to work with an existing document, you need to open it. All you do is pull down the File menu and select the Open command (or simply press **Ctrl+O**) to display the Open File dialog box. Now type the full name of the file into the Filename box. If the file is in a different drive or directory, be sure to include the drive letter and/or the directory name. When you're ready, select the **OK** button or just press **Enter**.

The shortcut key for opening a document in version 5.2 is **F4**. In the Open File dialog box, highlight the file you want and select the **O**pen button.

For more information on the Open command, see Chapter 7, "Day-to-Day Drudgery I: Saving, Opening, and Closing." To learn more about dialog boxes, see Chapter 6, "Talking to WordPerfect for Windows' Dialog Boxes."

4. Saving a File

One of the most gut-wrenching experiences in computerdom occurs when you work on a document for hours, and then lose everything because of a system crash or power failure. You can minimize this damage by saving your work regularly; just pull down WordPerfect for Windows' File menu and select the **Save** command, or press **Ctrl+S**. If you're saving a new file, the Save As dialog box will appear. Use the Filename box to give the file a name. When you're ready, select **OK**.

In version 5.2, press **Shift+F3** to save a file. If the Save As dialog box appears, enter the file name in the Save **As** box and then select the Save button.

See Chapter 7, "Day-To-Day Drudgery I: Saving, Opening, and Closing," for more details about saving your work.

5. Marking a Block of Text

Much of what you do in WordPerfect for Windows—whether it's cutting, copying, formatting, or printing—involves highlighting a block of text beforehand. Here's how you do it:

☞ With the keyboard, position the cursor to the left of the first character in the block, hold down the **Shift** key, and then use the arrow keys (or Page Up and Page Down if you have a lot of ground to cover) to highlight the block.

☞ With the mouse, point at the first character in the block, and then drag the mouse to move the pointer over the block.

You'll find lots more block info in Chapter 10, "Block Partying: Working with Blocks of Text." To learn how to drag a mouse, see Chapter 4, "Keyboard and Mouse Basics."

6. Formatting Characters

To make your documents stand out from the crowd, use WordPerfect for Windows' *character formatting* commands. With these commands you can

In WordPerfect for Windows 5.2, pull down the **Font** menu and select the appropriate command, or press **F9** and choose your options from the Font dialog box.

do simple formats like **bold** and *italics*, but you can also get into fancy stuff like different fonts, outlining, and shadowing. Just pull down the **Layout** menu and select the Font command (or press **F9**), and then choose the options you want from the Font dialog box that appears.

You can find the full scoop on all this in Chapter 12, "Making Your Characters Look Good."

7. Undoing a Mistake

The WordPerfect for Windows programmers thoughtfully included an Undo command that you can use to reverse your most recent action. This is great if you've just made a formatting gaffe, or if you "cut" something when you should have "copied" it. To use the Undo feature, just pull down the Edit menu and select the Undo command (or you can simply press **Ctrl+Z**).

But wait, there's more. WordPerfect for Windows also has an Undelete feature that can get you out of trouble if you've just deleted your entire day's work. To use it, first select U**ndelete** from the Edit menu (or press **Ctrl+Shift+Z**). Your most recent deletion will appear highlighted in the text, and the Undelete dialog box will appear. Select the **Restore** button

The shortcut key for the Undo command in version 5.2 is **Alt+Backspace**. For Undelete, press **Alt+Shift+Backspace**.

to restore the highlighted text. Select **Previous** or **Next** to take a look at the other stored deletions (WordPerfect for Windows stores the last three deletions). When you have the text you want, select **Restore**.

You'll learn about Undo in Chapter 10, "Block Partying: Working with Blocks of Text," and you'll learn about Undelete in Chapter 9, "Deleting Text (and Undeleting It, Too)."

8. Printing a File

Once you've finished working with a document, you'll want to print a copy to show your friends and colleagues. To do this, pull down the **File** menu and select the Print command (or press **F5**). The Print dialog box appears; it enables you to specify how much of the document to print, the number of copies, and various other settings. When you're ready to print, select the Print button.

For more printing particulars, take a look at Chapter 16, "Getting It Down on Paper: Printing Documents."

9. Checking Your Spelling

People are so picky these days that they'll often write off a document (and the person who wrote it) just because of a simple spelling mistake. To avoid this ignominious fate, take advantage of Speller—WordPerfect for Windows' built-in spell checker.

To run Speller, select the **Speller** command from the Tools menu and, in the dialog box that appears, select the **Start** button. WordPerfect for Windows laboriously checks every word in your document and displays any word it doesn't recognize, along with a suggested replacement. Select **Replace** to replace the word.

Speller is a powerful program with all kinds of fun options. To get all the facts, you need to turn to Chapter 20, "Using the Spell Checker and Thesaurus."

10. Quitting WordPerfect for Windows

When you've finished with WordPerfect for Windows, you can quit the program by pulling down the File menu and selecting the Exit command (or by pressing **Alt+F4**). If you've made changes to any open documents, WordPerfect for Windows will ask if you want to save them. Select Yes to save changes, or No to exit without saving.

See Chapter 3, "Diving In: Your First WordPerfect for Windows Session," for some additional stuff on quitting WordPerfect for Windows.

This page unintentionally left blank.

Chapter 2
Word Processing: A Primer

In This Chapter

- ☛ What is word processing?
- ☛ Is word processing a good thing?
- ☛ How does WordPerfect f̶ ̶ ̶ ̶ ̶ ̶ws fit in?
- ☛ What's new with ver̶ ̶
- ☛ The author gets s̶ ̶

Word processing. Per̶ ̶ ̶ ̶ so cold
and so, well, comp̶ ̶ ̶ ̶k does
that mean? The b̶ ̶ ̶ ̶. Who
processes word̶ ̶ ̶ ̶isspell
them, forget̶ ̶

But the comp̶ ̶ ̶at's what it
should be called, s̶ ̶ ̶te these misgiv-
ings, this chapter takes̶ ̶ ̶ssing thing. What is
it? What can you do with r̶ ̶

What Is You-Know-What?

Well, in the most basic, watch-their-eyes-glaze-over terms, *word processing* is using a computer to write, edit, format, and print documents. Yeah, I know, it doesn't sound very glamorous, but it's not really supposed to be. I mean, think about it. Most of the writing we do is grunt work anyway: memos, letters, essays, diatribes, and harangues of one sort or another. All we really need is to get the words down, dot the i's and cross the t's, make it presentable, and then get some hard copy that we can ship out. Everything else—whether it's putting together a newsletter or writing a doctoral thesis—is just an extension of this basic stuff.

Your Computer Is Not a Typewriter

All word processors have some kind of work area that you use for writing. Generally speaking, you just start pecking away on the computer's keyboard and the characters appear like magic on the screen.

Works just like a typewriter, right? Wrong. Oh sure, the keyboard looks somewhat familiar: the letters and numbers are arranged more or less the same, the spacebar is where it should be, and your old friends the Shift and Tab keys are there. Things may look the same but, baby, this ain't no Selectric.

The biggest difference, of course, is that the word processor has the muscle of a full-fledged computer behind it. Computers may be a lot dumber than we are (and don't let anyone tell you otherwise), but even the cheapest PC clone is way smarter than the most highfalutin' typewriter. For example, on a typewriter, a bell sounds to warn you when you near the end of a line. That's not bad, but the dumb beast still expects you to finish the line yourself and then press the Return key (or—gasp—crank the carriage return bar) to start a new line. A word processor, on the other hand, handles this chore for you. If you near the end of a line, you can blissfully continue typing, and the program will start a new line automatically. It'll even carry over any word you happen to be in the middle of.

Editing: Getting It Right

Word processors really begin to earn their stripes when it comes time to make changes in a document. With a typewriter, you can fix small mistakes, but you still have to fumble around with correction ribbons or (yuck) that ugly White-Out stuff. If you accidentally leave out a sentence or paragraph, forget about it. You've got to type the whole thing over.

Word processors, however, live to fix mistakes. Type the wrong character? Just press a button to delete it. Forget a paragraph? Just insert it where it needs to go. Want to move a section of text from the beginning of the document to the end? No problem: just "cut" it out and "paste" it in the appropriate place. Want to replace every instance of *affect* with *effect*? (I can never remember which is which, either.) Most word processors have a "search and replace" command that'll do just that.

And this is just the tip of the iceberg. A full-featured program, such as WordPerfect for Windows, has all kinds of strange and wonderful ways (including, thank goodness, a spell checker!) to get the job done right.

Formatting: Looking Good on Paper

Writing and editing are important of course, but the area where word processors really shine is *formatting*. It's not enough, in these image-conscious times, merely to hand someone a piece of paper with a bunch of words on it. Documents today need impact to get their message across. The formatting options in most word processors can help.

You can use **bold** to make things stand out, or *italics* for emphasis. You can center text or set tabs with just a few keystrokes. Some of the better programs also allow you to organize your words into columns, or wrap them around a picture. In the really high-end word processors (WordPerfect for Windows is one), you can even add cool features such as footnotes and tables of contents without breaking a sweat. If you can picture it in your head, you can probably do it with today's word processors.

Printing: Getting Hard Copy

Once you've finished changing a document, you'll need to print it out for others to see. It sounds like there wouldn't be much to this; just run some sort of "Print" command and the thing prints. But you have the choice of printing only certain parts of a document (a single page or even a single paragraph, for example) or printing multiple copies; or, if you have more than one printer, you choose which one you want to use. Some programs even let you see a page-by-page preview of what the document will look like.

Is Word Processing a Good Thing?

This may sound like a silly question to ask after extolling the numerous virtues of word processing programs. And it may be moot in any case, because word processing is by far the most popular category of computer software. Some people do have concerns, however, about what word processing is doing to our minds—so we may as well tackle those before going any further.

Problem #1: Word Processors Encourage Sloppy Writing

This is the most common problem put forth by so-called "writing experts." You usually hear three kinds of complaints:

- ☛ If a section of text doesn't work for some reason, people using word processors don't rewrite the whole thing from scratch. Instead, in trying to get the point across, they tend to insert more words and sentences. The usual result is bloated, overexplained thoughts that ramble incoherently.

- ☛ Most word-processor screens show only about half a page at a time, so people tend to see the trees (words, sentences, and paragraphs) instead of the forest (the entire document). As a result, word processing documents tend to lack organization, and they scatter separate pieces of the overall argument willy-nilly.

- ☛ The advent of the electronic thesaurus has made it easier to utilize cumbrous, orchidaceous words that serve only to obfuscate intendment and subjugate perspicuity.

My answer to these charges is that word processors don't write sloppily, *people* do. Forthwith, some suggestions you can use to avoid sloppiness in your own prose:

- ☛ Wherever possible, read your text out loud. If it doesn't flow off your tongue, it won't flow through someone's brain.

- ☞ If a sentence or paragraph doesn't feel right, try rewriting it from scratch instead of patching it up. If you can't bring yourself to delete it, at least move it off the screen where you can't see it (and so won't be influenced by it).

- ☞ A good word processor (such as WordPerfect for Windows) has outlining features that can help you organize large documents. This is a bit of an advanced topic, but it's worthwhile to learn before starting on that new novel.

- ☞ The best writing is clear and straightforward, without a lot of pretentious words that confuse more than they impress.

Problem #2: Word Processors Waste Time

You could see this one coming. Today's top-of-the-line word processors have so many bells and whistles that you can end up spending all your time fussing about with obscure fonts and complicated desktop publishing features. People often compound the problem by printing the document every time they make the slightest change. This just wastes paper and consumes valuable natural resources.

Again, these are behavioral problems, not word processor problems. On the one hand, it really is best to leave your work simple and uncluttered with fancy elements. This will keep your documents readable and your meaning clear. On the other hand, the best way to get familiar with any kind of software is to experiment with different features, and try out whatever looks interesting. You won't wreck anything, and most programs will warn you if you're about to do anything disastrous. And besides, you've got to have *some* fun.

Programs that come fully loaded with complicated options are called *fritterware* because you often end up frittering away your time playing around with the fun stuff instead of getting any work done.

Problem #3: Word Processors Create Illiterates

The same people who complained that calculators would turn our kids into math dropouts are now crying that computer spell checkers and grammar checkers will turn us all into illiterate slobs who wouldn't know a participle if it was dangled in front of us.

This one's easy to answer, folks: nuts to them, I say! If we can get our machines to handle the rote work of spelling and grammar, then I'm all for it. After all, meaning is what's most important. Why not take the time that we would normally spend with our noses in dusty dictionaries and use it to craft our concepts and polish our prose?

How Does WordPerfect for Windows Fit into All This?

If word processing was boxing (and on those days when our computers make us feel like putting our fist through our screens, I suppose it *is* something like the sweet science), a puny program like NotePad (the text editor that comes with Windows) would be in the flyweight division and Write (the more full-featured word processor that you also get free with Windows) would be a middleweight. This means that a muscular program like WordPerfect for Windows would have to be a heavyweight, because there are few chores this software can't handle.

As you'll soon see, WordPerfect for Windows has something for everyone. If all you need is basic editing features for things like letters and memos, WordPerfect for Windows will handle these chores with a few simple commands. If you need to put together large, complex documents, WordPerfect for Windows has features such as outlining, indexing, and footnotes that'll handle the biggest job without complaint. If your interests lie more toward desktop publishing (creating newsletters, brochures, and the like), WordPerfect for Windows can do page layout, columns of text, and graphics with the best of them. In other words, WordPerfect for Windows works the way you do, not the other way around.

What You See Is What You Get

One of the biggest advantages of WordPerfect for Windows (especially if you've ever used a DOS word processor) is that it operates in what is known as *graphics mode*. This means that when you format your documents (such as making characters bold or italic, or using different fonts), you can see the changes right on the screen, instead of having to wait for a printout.

With WordPerfect for Windows, what you see on your screen is what you get when it's printed. This not only saves time when formatting and laying out your documents, but it also saves trees because you don't have to print out every little change to see if it looks right.

What's New in Version 6?

Version 6 is a vastly changed product from its predecessors. It brings to the table several new features that put the program in line with some industry standards (such as pressing **Ctrl+Z** to undo your last action) and make the program both easier to use and more powerful. Here's a quick summary of some of the new features:

- ☞ QuickMenus that give you easy access to commands related to specific features.

- ☞ An improved status bar that you can customize to suit your needs.

- ☞ A two-page view that lets you see two pages on the screen at once.

- ☞ A new Power Bar that gives you easy access to the commands and features you use most often.

- ☞ A dozen different Button Bar layouts that let you tailor the Button Bar to the task you're working on.

- ☞ A Quick Format feature that lets you apply text-formatting options easily.

- ☞ QuickFinder, a new utility that lets you find your documents quickly.

- ☞ Improved tools for working with tables.

This book covers most of these new version 6 features, but don't feel left out if you have an older incarnation of the program. Any major differences in version 5.2 are spelled out in separate sidebars for handy reference.

SPEAK LIKE A GEEK

The ability to see on your computer screen what you end up getting from your printer is called *WYSIWYG* (What-You-See-Is-What-You-Get). It's pronounced "wizzy wig." (I swear I'm not making this up.)

The Least You Need to Know

This chapter took you on a quick tour of the shiny, happy world of word processing. Here's a recap of some of the sights we saw along the way:

- ☞ Word processing is a dumb name for using a computer to write, edit, format, and print documents.

- ☞ Your keyboard may look like a typewriter but, thanks to the computer in the box behind it, it's a lot smarter and a lot easier to use than a typewriter. Most editing and formatting commands are just a few keystrokes or mouse clicks away.

- ☞ Word processing is a good thing if you approach it the right way. Keep things simple, use the program's features to make your life easier, and don't be afraid to experiment.

- ☞ WordPerfect for Windows is the most popular word processor by far, because it works the way you do. Version 6 has all kinds of cool new features that'll keep you entertained for hours.

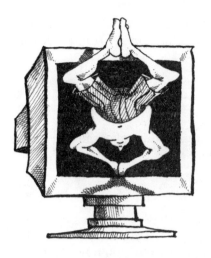

Chapter 3

Diving In: Your First WordPerfect for Windows Session

In This Chapter

☞ Starting WordPerfect for Windows

☞ Taking a tour around the screen

☞ Entering text

☞ Exiting WordPerfect for Windows

☞ A heartwarming story about skiing

The first time I ever went skiing, my friends (who, of course, were all experts and had little patience for a rank beginner) took me for a couple of token runs down the baby hill and then whisked me to the top of some huge mountain. (With friends like these! . . .)

In our travels down the mountain, we'd often come upon the steep, mogul-filled hills that my friends loved. These suckers scared the heck out of me, so I'd just follow everyone else, and I always made it down somehow. But I'd usually see groups of skiers standing at the top of these hills, fidgeting nervously, afraid to go down, but not able to turn back. In honor of these nervous-nellies, I developed my skiing motto: "Better a leg broken by boldness than a spirit broken by fear."

I tell you this story now, as we stand at the edge of the WordPerfect for Windows Hill, to inspire you to, as the ads say, "just do it." Follow my lead and we'll get through without a hitch.

Preflight Checklist

Before starting WordPerfect for Windows, you should make sure you've got everything you need. Here's a quick checklist:

Is Your Computer On?

This is, of course, important. Make sure not only that your computer is up and running, but that you've powered up anything else you'll need (such as your monitor or printer).

Is WordPerfect for Windows Installed?

If the program hasn't yet been installed, you have two choices:

☞ Find the nearest computer guru and ask him or her to install the program for you. This is the easiest method (for you, anyway), and you'll find most gurus can be easily cajoled with flattery ("Say, that's a *nice* pocket protector!").

☞ If you can't find a guru or you'd like to give it a go yourself, you'll find WordPerfect's installation program to be friendlier than most. First off, start Windows. Then insert the disk that's labeled Install 1 in the appropriate drive (usually A or B), select the **Run** command from the File menu in Windows, type **A:INSTALL** (or **B:INSTALL**, depending on which drive the disk is in), and press **Enter**. Then just follow the prompts on the screen.

Are You in Windows?

Before you can start WordPerfect for Windows, you need to have Windows started. (This assumes, of course, that Windows is installed on your computer. If it's not, go shell out an extra $75 or so and buy it, because WordPerfect for Windows is useless without it.)

If you see a box on your screen that says "Program Manager" at the top, you're in Windows. Otherwise, from the DOS prompt (which looks like C> or C:\> or some variation on this theme), type **WIN** and press **Enter**.

By the Way . . .

If you don't see anything that looks like Windows or the DOS prompt, you're likely in some other program. Here are some possibilities:

☞ The MS-DOS Shell program. If you see the words "MS-DOS Shell" at the top of your screen, hold down your keyboard's **Alt** key and press **F4** to return to DOS.

☞ Some kind of menu system. Your computer might be set up with a menu system that gives you a list of programs to run. If you're lucky, you may see a Windows option. If so, great! Just select the option to start Windows. Otherwise, look for an option called "Exit to DOS," or "Quit," or something similar. You can also try pressing the **Esc** key.

Is the Ambiance Just Right?

Make sure your surroundings are comfortable and your favorite computer accessories are nearby (a good, strong cup of coffee, relaxing background music, a copy of *Feel the Fear and Do It Anyway*, etc.).

The Three-Step Program for Starting WordPerfect for Windows

By the Way . . .

With Windows loaded, you should now see a box on your screen that says "Program Manager" at the top. If you don't, find the nearest guru and tell her that some dork in a book wants you to be in Program Manager. Better yet, why not learn how to do it yourself by picking up a copy of *The Complete Idiot's Guide to Windows* by the same dork? (Ah, yes, that *was* a shameless plug, wasn't it?)

Without further ado, here are the steps you need to follow to get WordPerfect for Windows up and running:

1. Hold down the **Alt** key on your keyboard and then tap **W**. You'll see a menu of options appear.

2. Look for an option named WPW in 6.0 (or, possibly, **WordPerfect**) and press the number you see beside it.
   This displays a box called "WPWin 6.0" (or "WordPerfect," in version 5.2), as shown on the next page.

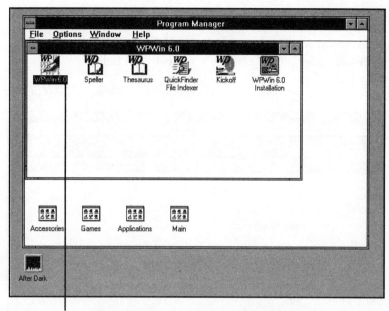

Select this icon to start WordPerfect for Windows.

You start WordPerfect for Windows by somehow selecting the WPWin 6.0 picture.

3. Look inside the WPWin box for a little picture labeled "WPWin 6.0" (or just "WPWin" for version 5.2 users). You start WordPerfect for Windows by "selecting" this picture, like so:

    ☞ With a mouse, move the pointer so it rests on the picture, and then press the left button twice quickly in succession.

    Or

    ☞ With your keyboard, press the arrow keys until the "WPWin 6.0" label is highlighted. Then press **Enter**.

The boxes you see (such as Program Manager and WordPerfect) are called *windows*. The little pictures you see infesting Program Manager's boxes are called *icons*.

Checking Out the WordPerfect for Windows Screen

WordPerfect for Windows will take a few seconds to crank itself up to speed. When it finally does, you'll see the screen shown below.

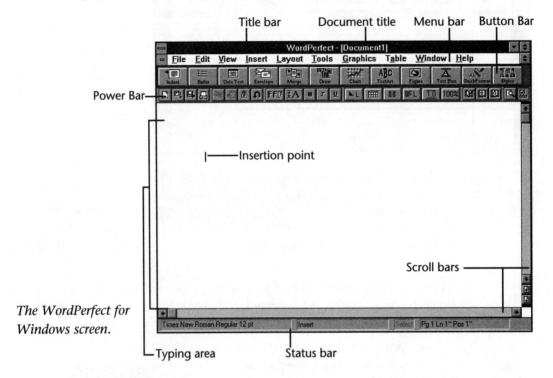

The WordPerfect for Windows screen.

The WordPerfect for Windows screen is somewhat stark, but it's not empty. Here's a quick rundown of what's there:

☛ **The typing area**   This is the large, blank expanse that covers most of the screen. This is where it all happens; everything you type will appear in this area. Think of it as the digital equivalent of a blank sheet of paper.

☛ **The insertion point**   This small, blinking line has a single purpose in life: it tells you where the next character you type will appear. Go ahead and press a letter on your keyboard. See how it shows up on the screen right where the insertion point was? The insertion point itself leaps ahead to tell you where your next character will appear. (Press **Backspace** to get rid of the character you typed.)

☛ **The title bar**　This area (besides reminding you that you're using WordPerfect) tells you the name of the current document. This is important because WordPerfect for Windows lets you have a bunch of documents open at the same time (yes, there *are* times when this is useful). This area also gives you helpful hints about what WordPerfect for Windows' commands and buttons mean.

☛ **The menu bar**　This is the second line from the top of the screen (File, Edit, View, etc.). Although you'd never know to look at it, this innocuous-looking line is actually your gateway to every single WordPerfect for Windows feature. This prodigious feat is accomplished by the miracle of pull-down menus. You'll learn all about these magical beasts in Chapter 5, "Using WordPerfect for Windows' Pull-Down Menus."

☛ **The Button Bar**　Below the menu bar, you'll find the Button Bar. Each "button" represents a specific WordPefect for Windows operation (such as indenting text). To learn how to use this handy feature, see Chapter 19, "Cool Tools to Make Your Life Easier."

☛ **The Power Bar**　Lying beneath the Button Bar, this feature—it's new in version 6.0—will without a doubt make your life easier. Each of the little squares you see represents a commonly used WordPerfect for Windows task (such as saving a file). A simple click of the mouse is all it takes to run any one of these buttons. I'll give you the details on using the Power Bar in Chapter 4, "Keyboard and Mouse Basics."

☛ **Scroll bars**　These things make it easy to navigate your longer documents with a mouse. See Chapter 8, "Day-to-Day Drudgery II: Navigating Documents," for the full lowdown.

☛ **The status bar**　Bars, bars, and more bars! This one gives you information about your document that you'll usually ignore, but it's nice to know it's there. The left side tells you things like the current font. The stuff on the right side looks pretty incomprehensible, doesn't it? The information is actually quite useful, although you probably won't appreciate it until you've used the program a bit. Here's a summary of what's there:

Info	What It Means
Pg 1	This is the page number you're on (Pg 1, Pg 2, and so on).
Ln 1"	This tells you which line the insertion point is on. The position is measured in inches (that's what the double-quote symbol (") means) from the top of the page. It starts at 1" because you have a one-inch margin at the top of the page.
Pos 1"	This tells you which column the insertion point is in. The position is measured in inches from the left edge of the page. Again, it starts at 1" because there's a one-inch margin on the left side of the page.

Margins are the (usually) empty areas that surround your text on the page. WordPerfect for Windows' standard margins are one inch high on the top and bottom, and one inch wide on the sides. See Chapter 14, "Making Your Pages Look Good," to learn how to change margin sizes.

Now What?

Okay, you've got this big-bucks word processor loaded, the insertion point is blinking away insistently, the large, blank typing area seems to cry out to be filled with happy little characters. What else do you need to know before getting started? Well, in a word, nothing! That's right, just start pecking away on your keyboard, and your brilliance will be displayed for all to see. This is the beauty of WordPerfect for Windows (if beauty is the right term): the program gets out of your way so you can get down to the business of writing.

Here are a few things to watch for when typing:

- ☞ If you're used to typing with a typewriter, you may be tempted to press the Enter key when you approach the end of a line. Fortunately, you don't have to bother, because WordPerfect for Windows handles that chore for you. When you've filled up a line, WordPerfect for Windows moves the text onto the next line automatically. Even if you're smack in the middle of a word, the program will automatically truck the entire word onto the next line, no questions asked. The only time you need to press Enter is when you want to start a new paragraph.

- If you make a mistake, just press the **Backspace** key to wipe it out. (If you don't see any key with the word Backspace on it, look for a left-pointing arrow (←) on the right end of the row with all the numbers.)

The feature that starts a new line automatically is called *word wrap*.

- As you type, some of the stuff in the status bar will change. As you move across the screen, the column position (Pos) will increase, and as you move to a new line, the row position (Ln) will increase.

- If you're entering a lot of text, you may be startled to see a line suddenly appear across the screen. No, there's nothing wrong with your screen. It just means that you've moved to a second page, and to show you where one page ends and the next begins, WordPerfect for Windows displays a line. As proof that you're on a new page, check out the status bar: WordPerfect for Windows bumps the page number (Pg) up to 2, and resets the line position to 1" (since you're now at the top of a new page).

This page-divider line is called a *page break*.

Getting Help

If you run into a problem with WordPerfect for Windows, or if you simply find yourself in a strange part of town, you want to get help fast before panic sets in. Thoughtfully, the WordPerfect programmers have provided you with a handy, on-line Help system. You start this system in one of two ways:

- Press **F1** to get help that is *context-sensitive*. This means the help screen that appears is related to whatever task you're in the middle of.

- Select a command from the **Help** menu. (You can display the Help menu by holding down **Alt** and pressing **H**.)

I won't go into the details of the Help system here. However, if you think you'll be using it regularly, Chapter 5, "Using WordPerfect for Windows' Pull-Down Menus," and Chapter 6, "Talking to WordPerfect for

Windows' Dialog Boxes," will tell you everything you need to know to navigate the Help system's windows. (By the way, to close a Help window, hold down **Alt** and press **F4**.)

Exiting WordPerfect for Windows

I know, I know, you're just starting to have fun, and here I am telling you how to exit the program. Well, you've gotta do it sometime, so you may as well know the drill:

1. Begin by pressing **Alt+F** (hold down the **Alt** key, press **F**, and then release both). You'll suddenly see a big list of stuff appear on your screen. This is your first look at one of the pull-down menus that I mentioned earlier.

> ## By the Way . . .
>
> In many places in this book, you'll see two keys separated by a plus sign, such as **Alt+F** in step 1. The plus sign means hold down the first key, press the second key, and then release both keys.

You can skip steps 1 and 2 by simply pressing **Alt+F4**.

2. Ignore everything you see except the line near the bottom of the list that says Exit. There are several ways to select this command, but for now, the easiest is simply to press X. If you've made changes to any open documents, WordPerfect for Windows will ask if you want to save them.

3. You have three choices at this point:

    ☞ If you don't want to save your changes, press **N** (for No).

    ☞ If you do want to save your changes, press **Y** (for Yes). If you see a box titled Save As, type a name that is eight letters or less (for now, don't use any punctuation marks or spaces in the name; see Chapter 7 for details on what is and isn't legal in creating a file name), and then press **Enter**.

☞ If you change your mind and decide you don't want to exit after all, just press the **Escape** key.

4. If you've made changes to more than one document, you may have to repeat step 3 a few times.

The Least You Need to Know

In this chapter, you made the big leap and learned how to start WordPerfect for Windows. The rest of the chapter wasn't terribly strenuous (I hope), but here's a quick summary anyway:

☞ Before starting WordPerfect for Windows, make sure Windows is loaded.

☞ In Program Manager, select the WPWin 6.0 window and then select the WPWin 6.0 icon.

☞ To enter text, just start typing. Remember that you don't have to press Enter at the end of each line.

☞ To exit WordPerfect for Windows, hold down **Alt**, press **F**, and then press **X** (or just press **Alt+F4**). If the program asks if you want to save your changes, select **Yes** or **No**, or press **Escape** to cancel.

This page unintentionally left blank.

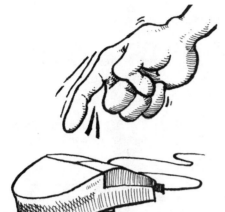

Chapter 4
Keyboard and Mouse Basics

In This Chapter

- ☛ A tour around the keyboard
- ☛ WordPerfect for Windows keyboarding basics
- ☛ The mouse made easy
- ☛ Musings on the ins and outs of garbage

"Garbage in, garbage out." That's an old expression computer geeks like to use to explain why things go haywire in software programs. Feed computers junk, and you get junk back because the dumb beasts just aren't smart enough to know the difference. In other words, input is everything.

When using WordPerfect for Windows, you have two ways to *input* stuff (that is, put stuff into your computer): the keyboard and the mouse. You don't have to become a keyboard connoisseur or a mouse maven to use WordPerfect for Windows, but to avoid the "garbage in" thing, it helps to digest a few basics. This chapter tells you all you need to know.

The Keyboard: A Guided Tour

Keyboards come in all shapes and sizes; like the proverbial snowflakes, it seems no two are alike. They all share a few common features, however, and most are laid out more or less the way you see in the picture below.

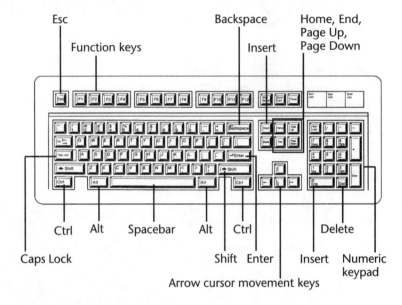

A typical PC keyboard. Just to be a pain, your computer manufacturer may have put the keys in slightly different positions.

Letters, Numbers, and Other Strangers

The bulk of the keyboard is taken up by the basic letters, numbers, punctuation marks, and other special characters that you'll be using most often (and some, like ~ and ^, that you may never use).

By the Way . . .

Typing teachers always suggest limbering up your fingers before getting down to heavy typing. One of the best ways to do this is to type out *pangrams*—sentences that use all 26 letters of the alphabet. The standard pangram that everybody (sort of) knows is *The quick brown fox jumps over the lazy dog.* This is fine, but it's a bit dull. Try some of these on for size:

Pack my box with five dozen liquor jugs.
The five boxing wizards jump quickly.
Judges vomit; few quiz pharynx block.
Sexy zebras just prowl and vie for quick, hot matings.

Shift and Caps Lock

Just like a typewriter, you use the Shift key to get capital letters. For keys with two symbols (except the ones on the numeric keypad; I'll talk about those later), hold down **Shift** to get the upper symbol. If you want to type nothing but capital letters for a stretch, it's better to press the **Caps Lock** key (similar to a typewriter's Shift Lock key). This only works for letters; to get the other symbols (such as **$** and **+**), you still need to use **Shift**. When you want to switch back to normal letters, press **Caps Lock** again.

The area of the keyboard that contains the letters, numbers, and punctuation keys is called the *alphanumeric keypad*.

Ctrl, Alt, and Those Bizarre WordPerfect Key Combinations

If you press **Ctrl** (it's pronounced "control") or **Alt**, nothing much happens, but that's okay because nothing much is supposed to happen. You don't use these keys by themselves, but as part of *key combinations*. (The Shift key often gets into the act as well.)

Let's try an example so you can see what I mean. Hold down the **Ctrl** key with one hand, use the other to tap the **W** on your keyboard, and then release **Ctrl**. Like magic, you'll see a box titled **WordPerfect Characters** appear on your screen. The point of this exercise isn't to do anything with this box (which you can get rid of by pressing the **Esc** key; or turn to Chapter 12 to figure out what it does), but to show you that you can get WordPerfect's attention simply by entering certain combinations of keys. Using the **Ctrl** and **W** combo is like saying, "Hey, I wanna see the WordPerfect Characters box on the screen!"

By the Way . . .

WordPerfect for Windows has all kinds of these strange-but-useful key combinations, so we need some kind of shorthand for verbose instructions like "Hold down the **Ctrl** key, tap **W**, and then release **Ctrl**." From now on, instead of this mouthful, I'll just say, "Press **Ctrl+W**."

The Esc Key

If you find yourself in some strange WordPerfect for Windows neighborhood, and you're not sure what to do next, you can usually get back to Kansas not by clicking your ruby slippers, but by pressing the **Esc** key until things look more familiar.

The Insertion Point Movement Keys

One of the principal differences between a word processor and a typewriter is that the word processor lets you leap around to any place in the document to fix blunders or just to check things out. You do this with the *insertion point movement* keys, which you'll find either on a separate keypad or mixed in among the numeric-keypad keys. You'll be learning all kinds of fun navigation stuff in Chapter 8, but for now, here's a quick summary of some basic insertion point movement techniques:

Press	To Move the Insertion Point
←	Left one character
→	Right one character
↑	Up one line
↓	Down one line
PageUp	To the top of the screen
PageDown	To the bottom of the screen

The Numeric Keypad

On each type of keyboard, the numeric keypad serves two functions. When the Num Lock key is on, you can use the numeric keypad to enter numbers. If Num Lock is off, the keypad's insertion point movement keys are enabled, and you can use them to navigate a document. Some keyboards (called *extended keyboards*) have a separate keypad for the insertion point movement keys so you can keep Num Lock on all the time.

The Function Keys

The *function keys* are located either to the left of the alphanumeric keypad, or across the top of the keyboard. There are usually 10 function keys (although some keyboards have 12), and they're labeled F1, F2, and so on. In Word-Perfect for Windows, you use these keys either by themselves or as part of key combinations. For example, the **Alt+F4** key combination is a quick way to exit WordPerfect for Windows.

If you press a key on the numeric keypad and, instead of getting a number, the insertion point moves, you have Num Lock turned off. Just tap the **Num Lock** key to enable the numbers. Most keyboards have a Num Lock indicator light that tells when Num Lock is on.

A Note About Notebook Keyboards

If you're ever forced to type for an extended period on a notebook or laptop keyboard, you have my deepest sympathies. These suckers are not only cramped, but they have all the feel of a piece of cement. To make things even worse, there's usually no separate numeric keypad, so the insertion point movement keys are scattered about willy-nilly. On some notebooks, the insertion point keys are hidden among the letters, and you have to hold down a special key (usually labeled "Fn") to get at them. Groan!

So what's my point? Well, just that you need to be a little more careful when using a notebook keyboard. Fingers that would normally fly (relatively speaking) on a regular keyboard will be bumping into each other in the cramped confines of the notebook layout. One solution that many notebooks offer is the capability of hooking up a separate numeric keypad—or even a full-fledged keyboard. You should check into this; it's definitely worth it.

WordPerfect for Windows Keyboarding for Non-Typists

As I've said, getting the most out of WordPerfect for Windows doesn't mean you have to become some kind of touch-typing, thousand-words-per-minute keyboard demon. Heck, I've been using computer keyboards for years, and I wouldn't know what touch-typing was if it bit me in the face. In this section, we'll just go through a few things that should make your life at the keyboard easier.

The Enter Key Redux

When you use a typewriter, a little bell goes off as you near the end of each line. This sound warns you to finish off the current word (or to add only a couple of small ones) and then press Return to start a new line. WordPerfect for Windows frees you from this old-fashioned drudgery; it starts new lines for you automatically. If you're smack in the middle of a word, this feature will even transport the whole word to the next line. So even though you ex-typewriter types may be sorely tempted to do so, *don't* press Enter as you near the end of a line. Just keep typing—WordPerfect will handle all the hard stuff. (You'll probably find you miss the little bell, though. Oh, well.)

SPEAK LIKE A GEEK

The feature that starts a new line automatically is called *word wrap*.

You can press **Enter** when you need to start a new paragraph. WordPerfect for Windows creates a new, blank line and moves the insertion point to the beginning of it.

You can also use Enter to insert blank lines in your text. Just position the insertion point at the beginning of a line, and press **Enter**. The new line appears above the current line.

Quick Fixes: Using Backspace and Delete

You'll be learning all kinds of fancy techniques for editing your documents in Part II. For now, though, you can use the Backspace and Delete keys to get rid of small typos. Just use the arrow keys to position the insertion point appropriately, and then use these keys as follows:

Backspace   Use this key to delete the character immediately to the left of the insertion point.

Delete   Use this key to delete the character immediately to the right of the insertion point.

Switching to Typeover Mode

If you position the insertion point in the middle of some text, anything you type gets inserted between the existing characters. (Why, yes, that *is* why they call it the *insertion* point.) If you're redoing a few words, you could delete them first and then retype, but usually it's easier to just type over them. To do this, you need to put WordPerfect for Windows in *typeover mode* by pressing the **Insert** key. (I know, I know, that doesn't make sense, but bear with me.) You'll see the word **Typeover** appear in the status bar, and when you type again, the new characters replace the existing ones. To resume normal operations, just press **Insert** again. As you may have guessed, the Insert key is a toggle, like a light switch—press it once and it's on; press it again and it's off.

Key Combination Contortions

WordPerfect for Windows has a key combination for just about anything you'd ever want to do with the program, and I'll be letting you in on some of them as we go through this book.

Most people find it faster to use one hand for these key combinations, but I'll warn you now to expect some real contortions. This is especially true for key combos that use either Ctrl or Alt and the function keys. Some of these nasty devils can be quite a stretch for all but the biggest hands. (Although things are made easier by some thoughtful computer companies that put Ctrl and Alt keys on both sides of the spacebar.) My advice? Don't strain yourself unnecessarily. Use two hands if you have to.

The problem with typeover mode is that, one of these days, you'll forget to turn it off, and you'll end up wiping out all kinds of important prose. When this happens, press **Ctrl+Z** (or **Alt+Backspace** if you have version 5.2) to undo the typeover, and then press **Insert** to return to the friendly confines of Insert mode.

Mouse Machinations

Learning how to use a mouse is by no means an essential WordPerfect for Windows survival skill. You'll find, however, that it makes many everyday tasks just plain faster and easier. The good news is that using a mouse takes no extraordinary physical skills. If you can use a fork without poking yourself in the eye, then you'll have no trouble wielding a mouse.

The Basic Mouse Technique

A mouse is a marvelous little mechanical miracle that can seem incomprehensible to the uninitiated. The basic idea, though, is simple: you move the mouse on its pad or on your desk, and a small pointer (see the screen shown below) moves correspondingly on your screen. By positioning the pointer on strategic screen areas, you can select text, operate the pull-down menus, and choose all kinds of WordPerfect for Windows options. Not bad for a rodent!

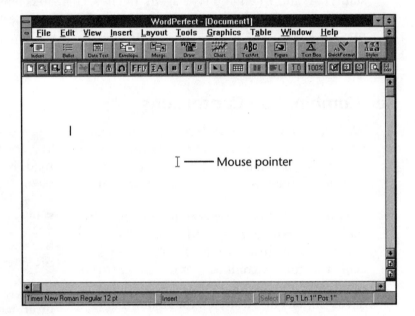

The WordPerfect for Windows mouse pointer.

By the Way . . .

If you don't see the mouse pointer on your screen, but you know you have a mouse installed, just wiggle the mouse a bit and the pointer should appear. WordPerfect for Windows always hides the pointer whenever you type something.

Using a mouse is straightforward, but it does take some getting used to. Here's the basic technique:

1. Turn the mouse so that its cable extends away from you.

2. Place your hand over the mouse in such a way that:

    ☞   the part of the mouse nearest you nestles snugly in the palm of your hand.

    ☞   your index and middle fingers rest lightly on the two mouse buttons. (If your mouse has three buttons, rest your fingers on the two outside buttons; leave the middle one alone for now.)

    ☞   your thumb and ring finger hold the mouse gently on either side.

3. Move the mouse around on its pad or on your desk. Notice how the mouse pointer on the screen moves in the same direction as the mouse itself.

The proper way to hold a mouse.

WordPerfect's Mouse Pointers

Just to make life confusing, WordPerfect for Windows will display a different mouse pointer for different tasks. Here are the four pointers you'll see most often:

I   This pointer appears inside the typing area.

    This pointer appears when you move the mouse into any of the regions surrounding the typing area (the title bar, menu bar, etc.).

⌛   This dreaded pointer appears when WordPerfect for Windows is busy with something. It means you won't be able to do anything until the program has finished its business.

↘   You use this pointer to change the size of some things.

The Hard Part: Controlling the Darn Thing!

While moving the mouse pointer is simple enough, controlling the pesky little thing is another matter. Most new mouse users complain that the pointer seems to move erratically, or that they move to one part of the screen and run out of room to maneuver. To help out, here are a few tips that will get you well on your way to becoming a mouse expert:

☞ Don't grab the mouse as if you were going to throw it across the room. (On occasion you may be tempted to actually throw it, but try to resist.) A light touch is all you need.

☞ The distance the mouse pointer travels on the screen depends on how quickly you move the mouse. If you move the mouse very slowly for about an inch, the pointer moves about the same distance (a little more, actually). However, if you move the mouse very fast for about an inch, the pointer leaps across the screen.

☞ If you find yourself at the edge of the mouse pad but the pointer isn't where you want it to be, simply pick up the mouse and move it to the middle of the pad. This doesn't affect the position of the pointer, but it does allow you to continue on your way.

Mouse Actions

Here's a list of the kinds of actions you can perform with a mouse:

Point   This means that you move the mouse pointer so it rests on a specific screen location.

Click   This means that you press and release the left mouse button once, quickly.

Right-click   Quickly press and release the right mouse button.

Double-click   As you might expect, double-clicking means that you quickly press and release the left mouse button twice in succession.

Drag   This has nothing to do with dressing funny. It simply means that you press and hold down the left mouse button, and then move the mouse.

The Least You Need to Know

This chapter gave you the lowdown on using the keyboard and mouse in WordPerfect for Windows. Here are a few highlights:

- ☞ You'll spend most of your typing time pecking out letters, numbers, and punctuation in the alphanumeric keypad.

- ☞ You use the **Ctrl** and **Alt** keys (and sometimes **Shift**) in combination with other keys to access WordPerfect's commands.

- ☞ The insertion point movement keys help you move around in a document. They appear in a separate keypad, or mixed in with the numeric keypad (in which case, you have to turn Num Lock off to get at them).

- ☞ Use the numeric keypad to enter numbers into your documents quickly. Make sure you turn **Num Lock** on before using these keys.

- ☞ The function keys are the 10 (or sometimes 12) keys labeled F1, F2, and so on. In WordPerfect for Windows, you use these either by themselves or in combination with other keys to run certain commands.

- ☞ A mouse can make WordPerfect for Windows easier to use, but it does take some getting used to.

This page unintentionally left blank.

Chapter 5

Using WordPerfect for Windows' Pull-Down Menus

In This Chapter

- ☞ What are pull-down menus?
- ☞ How to use pull-down menus with a mouse
- ☞ How to use pull-down menus with the keyboard
- ☞ Rambling ruminations on desks, drawers, and the Dead Sea Scrolls

You (or your company) didn't shell out the big bucks for WordPerfect for Windows so you could type all day. To get the most out of your investment, you need to use the program's other features. How do you access those features? Well, if you read the last chapter, then you know that one way is by using key combinations. But key combinations, while often quicker, have two major drawbacks:

- ☞ Either you have to memorize them (shudder) or you have to interpret WordPerfect's arcane keyboard template (a task akin to deciphering the Dead Sea Scrolls).
- ☞ They can be physically brutal unless you have basketball-player-sized hands.

Fortunately, there's an easier alternative: *pull-down menus*. They group commands in logical chunks, they're a snap to use (especially with a mouse), and you still maintain access to every WordPerfect for Windows feature. Sound good? Then read on, and I'll show you how they work.

What the Heck Are Pull-Down Menus?

Take a good look at the desk you're sitting at. (If you're not sitting at a desk, picturing one in your head will do.) You've probably got an area where you do your work, surrounded by various tools (pens, pencils, and so on) and things that keep you informed (such as a clock and calendar). You probably also see a few drawers, from which you get your work and in which you store your desk tools.

The WordPerfect for Windows screen is also a lot like a desk. You have the typing area to work in, of course, and you have the status bar to keep you informed. And you also have pull-down menus that work, in fact, just like desk drawers. When you need to get more work (that is, open a document) or access a WordPerfect for Windows command, you simply open the appropriate menu and select the menu option that runs the command.

Why You Pull Down Instead of Up or Out

Why are they called "pull-down" menus? Well, because they're hidden inside the menu bar near the top of the screen. Selecting any of the ten menu bar options (File, Edit, View, etc.) displays a menu of choices, such as the File menu shown below.

File	
New	Ctrl+N
Template...	Ctrl+T
Open...	Ctrl+O
Close	Ctrl+F4
Save	Ctrl+S
Save As...	F3
QuickFinder...	
Master Document	▶
Compare Document	▶
Document Summary...	
Document Info...	
Preferences...	
Print...	F5
Select Printer...	
Exit	Alt+F4

WordPerfect for Windows'
File pull-down menu.

The effect, you'll note, is as though you pulled the menu down from the menu bar. See, sometimes this stuff actually makes sense!

The choices you see listed in a pull-down menu are called *commands*. You use these commands to tell WordPerfect for Windows what you want it to do next.

How to Use Pull-Down Menus with a Mouse

If you have a mouse, using pull-down menus is a breeze. All you do is move the mouse pointer into the menu bar area (the pointer will change to an arrow), and then click on the name of the menu you want to pull down. For example, clicking on File in the menu bar pulls down the File menu.

Once you have a menu displayed, you need to select one of the commands. This is simple enough: you just click on the command you want to execute. Depending on the option you select, one of three things will happen:

☞ The command will be executed (at dawn).

☞ Another menu will appear. In this case, just click on the command you want to execute from the new menu.

☞ Something called a *dialog box* will appear to get further info from you. See Chapter 6, "Talking to WordPerfect for Windows' Dialog Boxes," for details on using dialog boxes.

How to Use Pull-Down Menus with the Keyboard

The secret to using pull-down menus from the keyboard is to look for the underlined letter in each menu bar option. For example, look at the "F" in File, the "E" in Edit, and so on. These underlined letters are the menu options' *hot keys*. How do they work? Simple: you just hold down **Alt**, and press the hot key on your keyboard. For example, to pull down the File menu, use the **Alt+F** key combination.

To select one of the commands, use the up and down arrow keys to highlight the command you want (a *highlight bar* moves up and down to mark the current command), and then press **Enter**. As I explained in the mouse section, one of three things will happen depending on which one you select:

☛ The command will be executed.

☛ Another menu will appear. In this case, use the arrow keys to select the command you want from the new menu, and then press **Enter**.

☛ A dialog box will appear, asking you for more information.

By the Way . . .

What do you do if you pull down a menu and discover you don't want to select a command? No problem. You have two choices:

☛ To return to the document, either click anywhere inside the document or press **Alt** by itself.

☛ To pull down a different menu, click on the menu name or press **Alt** plus the letter of the new menu.

More Fun Pull-Down Menu Stuff

If you've been pulling down some menus, you may have noticed a few strange things. For example, did you notice that some commands have a triangle on the right-hand side of the menu? Or that some are followed by three ominous-looking dots? Or that others also list a key (or key combination)? These are just a few of the normal features found in all pull-down menus, and you can take advantage of them to make your life easier. The rest of this section summarizes these features. I'll be using the Layout menu (shown on the next page) as an example, so you might want to pull it down now to follow along.

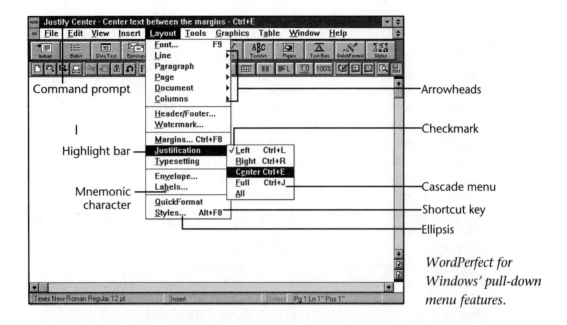

Command prompt

Highlight bar

Mnemonic character

Arrowheads

Checkmark

Cascade menu

Shortcut key

Ellipsis

WordPerfect for Windows' pull-down menu features.

Command Prompts: Helpful Hints

WordPerfect for Windows has so many commands that it's just about impossible (and probably not very useful) to remember what each one does. Fortunately, you don't have to, because whenever you highlight a command, WordPerfect displays a prompt in the title bar that gives you a brief description of the command. If this description seems reasonable, go ahead and select the command. If it doesn't, you're free to move on.

As a reminder, you highlight a command in a pull-down menu by using the up and down arrow keys to scroll through the list. Mouse users can get into the act as well, by using a slightly different technique for pulling down a menu. Move the pointer over the menu name, press the left mouse button and *hold it down*. Keep the button held down and move the mouse pointer through the menu commands. (This is called *dragging* the mouse.) As the pointer hits each command, the prompt appears in the title bar. To select a command, just release the mouse button while the command you want is highlighted. To remove the menu without selecting a command, move the pointer off the menu and then release the button.

In version 5.2, the command prompts appear in the status bar at the bottom of the screen.

Underlined Characters: More Hot Keys

Every command in a pull-down menu has
one underlined character. This means that
when you display the menu, you can select
any command by simply pressing its underlined letter on your keyboard. For example,
in the Layout menu, you could select, say,
the Font command simply by pressing **F**. (If
you're itching to try this out, go ahead and
press **F**. You'll eventually see a box named
Font on your screen. I'll be discussing font
stuff in Chapter 12, "Making Your Characters Look Good,"
so for now just press **Esc** to return to your document.)

The underlined characters in
pull-down menu commands
are called *selection letters*.

Shortcut Keys: The Fast Way to Work

Some menu commands also show a key or key
combination on the right-hand side of the menu.
These are called *shortcut keys*: they allow you to
bypass the menus altogether and activate a command quickly from your keyboard. For example,
you can select the Layout menu's **Margins** command simply by pressing
Ctrl+F8. (If you try this, press **Esc** to remove the Margins dialog box that
appears. To learn about working with page margins, see Chapter 14,
"Making Your Pages Look Good.")

By the Way . . .

Confusingly, the shortcut keys only work when you don't
have a menu displayed. If you press a key combination with a
menu pulled down, WordPerfect for Windows will ignore it
and wait for you to do something sensible.

Once you've worked with WordPerfect for Windows for a while, you
may find it faster to use these shortcut keys for the commands you use
most often.

Arrowheads (Menus, Menus, and More Menus)

With some commands, you'll see an arrowhead (▶) on the right side of
the menu. This tells you that yet another menu will appear when you
select this command. For example, select the Justification command from
the Layout menu to see a menu of commands for justifying text. (Press **Esc**
to remove the new menu. I'll talk about each of these commands in
Chapter 13, "Making Your Lines and Paragraphs Look Good.")

The Ellipsis (the Three-Dot Thing)

An *ellipsis* (...) after a command name indicates that a dialog box will
appear when you select the option. WordPerfect for Windows uses dialog
boxes to ask you for more information, or to confirm a command you
requested. For example, if you select the Layout menu's Font command, a
dialog box appears to find out what kind of font you want to use. (Press
Esc to remove this dialog box.) See Chapter 6, "Talking to WordPerfect for
Windows' Dialog Boxes," for more dialog box details.

Check Marks: The Active Command

Some menu commands exist only to turn certain features of the program
or a document off and on (like a light switch). For example, pull down the
View menu. You should see a check mark beside the Status Bar command.
This means that the status bar is currently visible. If you select this command, WordPerfect for Windows removes the status bar from the screen.
Pull down the View menu again, and you'll see there is no longer a check
mark beside Status Bar. Select the command again to turn the status bar
back on.

What You Can't Do: The Dimmed Options

You'll sometimes see menu options that appear in a lighter color than the
others. These are called *dimmed options* and the dimming indicates that
you can't select them (for now, anyway). If you see a dimmed option, it
usually means you must do something else with the program before the
option will become active.

Using Version 6's QuickMenus

Mouse users get an extra bonus in version 6: QuickMenus. These menus display a short list of commands related to a specific feature. All you do is place the mouse pointer over the feature and then right-click. When the menu appears, just click (the left button this time) on the command you want.

For example, if you right-click in the typing area (but not in any of the margins), you'll see the QuickMenu shown below. Notice how the options are all related to the text in a document. (To get rid of the QuickMenu, click anywhere in the typing area.)

*One of the
QuickMenus from
WordPerfect for
Windows version 6.*

QuickMenus are available for the following features (among others):

Text	Power Bar
Left margin	Status bar
Headers and footers	Scroll bars

The Least You Need to Know

This chapter explained WordPerfect for Windows' pull-down menus, and showed you how to use them with both a mouse and a keyboard. Here's a summary of what you now know:

☞ Pull-down menus are a lot like desk drawers, because they store tools (commands) that you use with WordPerfect for Windows.

☞ To pull down a menu with the mouse, simply click on the menu name in the menu bar.

- ☞ To pull down a menu with the keyboard, look for the menu's hot key and then, while holding down **Alt**, press the key on your keyboard.

- ☞ Once you pull down a menu, you can select a command by using your keyboard's up and down arrow keys to highlight the command, and then pressing **Enter**. If you have a mouse, just click on the command you want.

- ☞ QuickMenus (new in version 6) present you with a short list of commands related to a specific screen area. Right-click on the area to display its QuickMenu.

This page unintentionally left blank.

Chapter 6
Talking to WordPerfect for Windows' Dialog Boxes

In This Chapter

- ☞ What is a dialog box?

- ☞ Getting around in dialog boxes

- ☞ Learning about dialog box buttons, boxes, and lists

- ☞ Odd dialog box details that you might never have thought to ask about

As you work with WordPerfect for Windows, little boxes will appear incessantly on your screen to prompt you for more information (and generally just confuse the heck out of things). These are called *dialog boxes*, and they're WordPerfect's way of saying, "Talk to me!" This chapter looks at these chatty little beasts, and offers some helpful tips for surviving their relentless onslaught.

Where Do They Come From?

Dialog boxes may sometimes seem to appear out of nowhere, but they generally show up after you select certain options from WordPerfect for Windows' pull-down menus or press certain key combinations.

Whether or not a dialog box appears depends on whether or not the program needs more information from you. For example, if you select the File menu's Print command, WordPerfect for Windows displays the Print dialog box to ask you which printer to use, how many copies you want to print, and so on.

> ### By the Way . . .
> You can always tell when a command will generate a dialog box by looking for three dots (...) after the command name. These three dots (they're known as an *ellipsis*) tell you that some kind of dialog box will appear if you select the option. This gives you time to prepare yourself mentally for the ordeal to come.

Dialog Box Basics

Here are a few points about dialog boxes to keep in mind as you work through this chapter:

- Dialog boxes always have a title at the top of the box. This lets you know if you selected the right command.

- Dialog boxes like to monopolize your attention. When one is on the screen, you can't do other things, such as enter text in the typing area or select a pull-down menu. Deal with the dialog box first, and then you can do other things.

- The various objects you see inside a dialog box are called *controls* because you use them to control the way the dialog box works.

- Every control has a name that identifies it.

Navigating Controls

Before you learn how these controls operate, you need to be able to move among them. (This section applies only to keyboard users. Mouse users select a control merely by clicking on it.)

The first thing you need to be able to figure out is which control is currently selected. (This can be easy or hard depending on how many controls the dialog box has.) You need to look for one of two things:

☞ If the control displays text inside a box, the control is active either when the text is highlighted or when you see an insertion point cursor blinking on and off inside the box.

☞ All other controls display a dotted outline around their name when they're selected.

Think of these guidelines as "You are here" signs on a map and keep them in mind as you move through WordPerfect for Windows' dialog boxes.

Once you know where you are, you can move around by pressing **Tab** (which moves, more or less, top to bottom and left to right through the controls) or **Shift+Tab** (which moves bottom to top and right to left). Select **P**rint from the File menu and try some experiments in the Print dialog box. Each time you press Tab (or Shift-Tab), make sure you can find the selected control before moving on. Press **Esc** when you're done.

Working with Command Buttons

The most basic dialog box control is the *command button*. The dialog box shown below has four command buttons: OK, Cancel, Use as Default, and Help. (To display this dialog box, select Repeat from the Edit menu.) When you select a command button, you're telling WordPerfect for Windows to execute the command written on the face of the button.

Spinner ——
Command buttons ——

A command button executes the command written on its face.

To select a command button from the keyboard, press **Tab** until the command button you want is selected (that is, the button name is surrounded by a dotted outline) and then press **Enter**. To select a command button with a mouse, just click on the button.

WordPerfect for Windows uses command buttons for all kinds of things, but three are particularly common: OK, Cancel, and Help. Here's what they do:

 Select this button when you've finished with the dialog box and you want to put all your selections into effect. This is the "Make it so" button.

 Select this button to cancel the dialog box. It's useful for those times when you panic and realize that you're looking at the wrong dialog box or when you've made a mess of your selections. This is the "Belay that last order" button.

 Select this button when you haven't the faintest idea what you're doing and you'd like WordPerfect for Windows to give you a hint. This is the "Please explain" button.

Working with Edit Boxes

An *edit box* is a screen area you use to type in text information, such as a description or a file name. When you first select one, you'll see a blinking insertion point inside the box (if it's empty) or highlighted text (if it's not). The Document Summary dialog box shown below contains several edit boxes. (Selecting Document Summary from the File menu will display this dialog box.)

Edit boxes ——

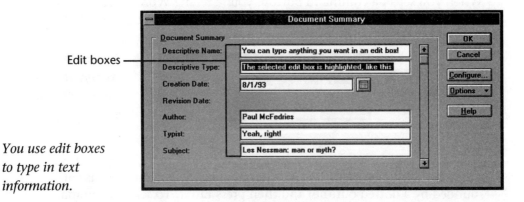

You use edit boxes to type in text information.

To use an edit box from your keyboard, press **Tab** either until you see the insertion point in the box or until you see the text in the box highlighted, and then begin typing. To use an edit box with a mouse, click anywhere inside the box and then type in your text. If you make any mistakes when typing, you can use the Backspace and Delete keys to expunge the offending letters.

By the Way . . .

When the text in an edit box is highlighted, it means that the text will be replaced by whatever you type. If you don't want to replace the entire text, just press either the left or right arrow key to remove the highlight, and then position the insertion point appropriately.

Working with Option Buttons

Option buttons are WordPerfect for Windows' equivalent of the old multiple-choice questions you had to struggle with in school. You're given two or more choices, and you're only allowed to pick one. In the dialog box shown below, there are three option buttons. (To access this dialog box, select Page from the Layout menu, and then select Center.) As you can see, an option button consists of a small circle with a label beside it that tells you what the option is.

Option buttons ⎯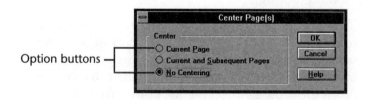

You can only select one option button at a time.

How do you activate an option button? From the keyboard, you need to press **Tab** until one of the option buttons is selected (it's name is surrounded by a dotted outline) and then you use the up and down arrow keys to pick out the one you want. Notice that a black dot appears inside the circle of the button that you activate.

If you have a mouse, simply click on the option you want (you can either click on the button itself or on the name).

If you're outside a group, you can still select a control inside the group quickly. Just hold down **Alt** and press the underlined letter in the control's name.

Understanding Dialog Box Groups

Most WordPerfect for Windows dialog boxes organize related controls into groups and surround them with a box. The Center Page(s) dialog box, for example, has a group called Center. When you're inside one of these groups, you can usually select another control in the group simply by pressing the underlined letter in the control. For example, in the Center group, you could select the Current Page control by pressing **P**.

Working with Spinners

Spinners are controls that let you scroll up or down through a series of numbers. For example, in the Repeat dialog box shown earlier, the **Number of Times to Repeat** control is a spinner.

Spinners have two parts:

☞ On the left you'll see an edit box that you can use to type in the number you want (boring).

☞ On the right you'll see two buttons with upward and downward pointing arrows. Click on the upward pointing arrow to increase the number shown in the edit box. Click on the downward pointing arrow to decrease the number. For some real fun, press and hold down the mouse button on one of the arrows and watch the numbers really fly!

Working with List Boxes

A *list box* is a small window that displays a list of items, such as file names or directories. A highlight bar shows the currently selected item in the list. The dialog box shown on the next page has two list boxes. (If you'd like to display this dialog box on your screen, pull down the Graphics menu and select the Figure command.)

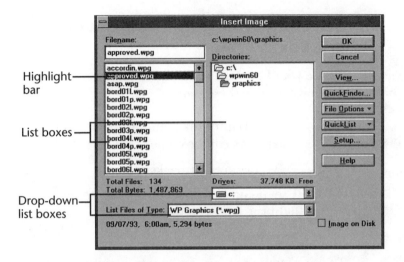

Highlight bar

List boxes

Drop-down list boxes

This dialog box has several examples of list controls.

To use a mouse to select an item from a list box, you can

☞ Click on the item if it's visible.

☞ Use the scroll bars, if necessary, to display the item, and then click on it. (If you're a little leery of those scroll bar things, see the section titled "A Brief Scroll Bar Primer," later in this chapter.)

To select a list box item using your keyboard, press **Tab** until an item in the list is selected (you'll see a dotted line around the item) and then use the up and down arrow keys (or Page Up and Page Down if the list is a long one) to highlight the item you want.

Working with Drop-Down Lists

A *drop-down list* is like a combination of an edit box and a pull-down menu. You can type in the option you want or you can select it from a list that drops down (hence the name) when you select it. Drop-down list boxes usually contain lists of related items, such as font names or document files. The Insert Image dialog box has two drop-down list boxes: List Files of Type and Drives.

Here's a spiffy tip that can save you oodles of time. Once you're inside a list box, press the first letter of the item you want. WordPerfect for Windows leaps down the list and highlights the first item in the list that starts with the letter you pressed. If you keep typing, WordPerfect tries to find any item that matches the letters you've entered.

TECHNO NERD TEACHES

The two list boxes shown in the Insert Image dialog box on the preceding page are slightly different. The **Directories** control is a pure list box. The **Filename** control, however, is technically called a *combination list box*, because it combines an edit box with a list box. This means that, besides selecting an item from the list, you could also type in what you want in the edit box.

Selecting Stuff from Drop-Down List Boxes

To use your keyboard to select an item from a drop-down list, follow these steps:

1.   Press **Tab** until the item inside the drop-down list's edit box is selected.

2.   Press the down arrow key to open the list.

3.   Use the up and down arrow keys to highlight the item you want.

4.   Press **Enter**.

To use a mouse to select an item from a drop-down list, follow these steps:

1.   Click on the downward-pointing arrow on the right side of the control. This opens the list to display its options.

2.   Click on the item you want. If you don't see the item you want, use the scroll bar to view more of the list. (If you're not sure how a scroll bar works, see the next section.)

A Brief Scroll Bar Primer

You'll be learning more about scroll bars in Chapter 8, but I'll give you a brief introduction here so you'll be able to use the drop-down lists.

Some lists contain too many items to fit inside the box. In this case, a scroll bar appears on the right hand side of the box to make it easier to navigate the list. The box inside the scroll bar (called, appropriately enough, the *scroll box*) tells you where you are in the list. For example, if the scroll box is halfway between the top and the bottom of the scroll bar, then you're approximately halfway down the list.

To navigate a list with the scroll bar, use the following mouse techniques:

☞   To scroll through the list one item at a time, click on either of the arrows at the top and bottom of the scroll bar.

☛ To jump quickly through the list, click inside the scroll bar between the scroll box and the top (to move up) or between the scroll box and the bottom (to move down).

☛ To move to a specific part of the list, drag the scroll box up or down.

Working with Check Boxes

The real world is constantly presenting us with a series of either/or choices. You're either watching Oprah or you're not; you're either eating Heavenly Hash or you're not. That kind of thing. Word-Perfect for Windows handles these sorts of yes-or-no, on-or-off decisions with a control called a *check box*. The check box presents you with an option that you can either activate (check) or not.

In the Font dialog box shown below (select Font from the Layout menu), the Appearance group contains no fewer than ten check boxes. As you can see, a check box consists of a small square and a label that tells you what the check box controls. You know a check box is activated when you see an "X" inside the square, and that it's deactivated when the square is empty.

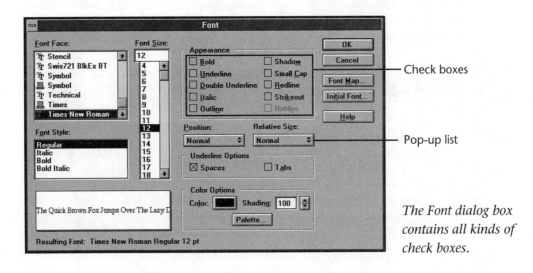

Check boxes

Pop-up list

The Font dialog box contains all kinds of check boxes.

To activate a check box from the keyboard, press **Tab** until the check box you want is selected and then press the **Spacebar**. To deactivate the check box, press the **Spacebar** again.

To activate a check box with a mouse, click on the box or on its name. To deactivate the box, just click on the box again.

Working with Pop-Up Lists

Pop-up lists are a cross between a command button and a list. Instead of showing a command name, the button face always shows the current selection from the list. In the Font dialog box shown on the preceding page, there are two pop-up lists: Position and Relative Size.

To work with a pop-up list from the keyboard, follow these steps:

1. Press **Tab** until you select the button name.

2. To scroll through the choices without popping up the list, just press the up or down arrow keys. To pop up the list, press either **Alt+up arrow** or **Alt+down arrow** (you'll see that the current selection has a check mark beside it). Then use the up and down arrow keys to highlight the item you want.

3. If you popped up the list, press **Enter** to select your choice.

With a mouse, place the pointer over the appropriate pop-up list and then press and hold down the left mouse button. When the list appears, keep the mouse button pressed and move the pointer up or down until the selection you want is highlighted. Then release the button.

The Least You Need to Know

This chapter showed you the ins and outs of using dialog boxes to communicate with WordPerfect for Windows. We covered a lot of ground and you learned all kinds of new things. If it's not all clear in your head right now, don't worry about it because, believe me, you'll be getting plenty of practice. In the meantime, here's some important stuff to remember:

☞ WordPerfect for Windows uses dialog boxes to ask you for more information or to confirm that the command you've selected is what you really want to do.

☞ Keyboard jockeys use the **Tab** key (or **Shift+Tab**) to move through the dialog box controls.

☞ Many controls have underlined letters. When you're in a group, you can select these controls by pressing the letter on your keyboard. Outside the group, you can select a control by holding down **Alt** and pressing the control's underlined letter.

☞ Most dialog boxes use the OK, Cancel, and **Help** buttons. Select OK to exit the dialog box and put your choices into effect. Select Cancel to bail out of a dialog box without doing anything. Select **Help** to find out just what the heck is going on.

This page unintentionally left blank.

Chapter 7
Day-to-Day Drudgery I: Saving, Opening, and Closing

In This Chapter

- Saving a document
- Saving a document under a different name
- Opening and retrieving a document
- Closing a document
- Cat waxing and other handy skills

WordPerfect for Windows, especially version 6, is jam-packed with power-ful features that let you do everything but wax the cat. But even with all that power at your fingertips, you still need to take care of mundane drudgery, such as opening and saving documents (the subject of this chapter) and navigating your way through large files (which I'll save for Chapter 8).

Save Your Work, Save Your Life

Most people learn about saving documents the hard way. For me, it was a power failure that wiped out an entire day's writing. Believe me, that kind of thing can make you old before your time.

Why is saving necessary? Well, when you open a document, WordPerfect for Windows copies it from its safe haven on your hard disk to the volatile confines of your computer's memory. When you shut off your computer (or if a power failure forces it off), everything in memory is wiped out. If you haven't saved your document to your hard disk, you'll lose all the changes you made.

Saving an Existing Document

Fortunately, WordPerfect for Windows makes saving your work as easy as shooting fish in a barrel. In fact, I can tell you the whole thing in a single sentence: To save the document you're working on, either pull down the File menu and select the **Save** command or just press **Ctrl+S** (**Shift+F3** in version 5.2). That's it!

You can also click on this tool in the Power Bar to save a document.

Save

What's Wrong with This Picture?

Saving your work is vital, but few people do it often enough. How often is often enough? Here's a quiz you can take to see if you know:

You should save your work if:

(a)   You have a delay while you think of what to say next (a common occurrence for many of us).

(b)   You've just entered a long passage.

(c)   You've just formatted a large section of text.

(d)   You've just rearranged a bunch of stuff.

(e)   You've just retrieved another document into the current one.

(f)   All of the above.

The answer, of course, is (f), All of the above. Saving is so easy that you really should do it as often as you can. Use (a) through (e) as guidelines for deciding when it's time to save.

Saving a New Document

Well, actually, there's a little more to this saving business than I've let on. If you're saving a new document, WordPerfect for Windows will need to know the name you want to use, so you'll see the Save As dialog box shown below.

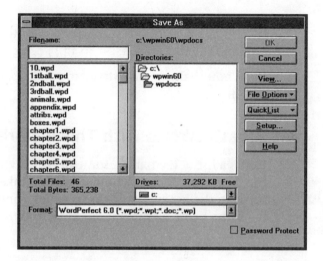

When you save a new document, WordPerfect for Windows displays the Save As dialog box so you can name the file.

Type a name in the Filename edit box (before you do, however, you should read the "Sacred File Name Commandments" section, below) and then select the **OK** button.

If you give the document the name of a file that already exists, WordPerfect for Windows will warn you, and ask if you want to replace the existing file. Replacing the file will mean it's gone for good—and no amount of hocus-pocus will get it back. So, unless you're sure you won't ever need the other file, select No and try again.

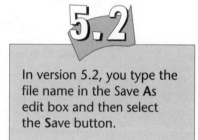

In version 5.2, you type the file name in the Save **As** edit box and then select the **S**ave button.

Sacred File Name Commandments

File names usually contain a period flanked by a *primary name* on the left and an *extension* on the right. When naming your documents, make sure you observe the sacred File Name Commandments handed down by the great DOS nerd gods:

I. Thou shalt not use more than eight characters for the file's primary name.

II. Thou shalt not use more than three characters for the file's extension.

III. Thou shalt separate the primary name and the extension with a period.

IV. Thou shalt not use a space or any of the other forbidden characters: + = \ | [ ] ; : , . < > ? /

V. Thou shalt not take the name of an existing file.

If you enter an illegal name, WordPerfect for Windows will display a dialog box that says **This file name is invalid.** Just press **Enter** or click on **OK** to return to the Save As dialog box and try again.

What's Wrong with This Picture?

Here's a list of file names, some of which violate the sacred File Name Commandments. Take a look through the list and write down which commandment the name blasphemes (if any), and the reason.

1. COWABUNGA.TXT

    Commandment violated:

    Reason:

2. WHATTHE.HECK

    Commandment violated:

    Reason:

3. NO_FRUIT.SIR

    Commandment violated:

    Reason:

    Answers:

4. IS THIS.OK?

    Commandment violated:

    Reason:

5. THISISIT

    Commandment violated:

    Reason:

6. DUH,SAID.HE

    Commandment violated:

    Reason:

1. Incorrect: This name violates Commandment I because the primary name is nine characters long.

2. Incorrect: Commandment II is violated because this name uses a four-character extension.

3. Correct: The underscore character (_) is legal, and it's useful for making file names more legible.

4. Incorrect: This name actually has two mistakes. The space in the primary name and the question mark in the extension both violate Commandment IV.

5. Correct: The extension is optional. (Notice that when there's no extension, you don't need the period.)

6. Incorrect: The comma in the primary name violates Commandment IV. The two-character extension is okay, though.

By the Way . . .

Even though extensions are optional, most people use them anyway because they're handy for identifying what type of file you're dealing with. If you don't give an extension, WordPerfect for Windows automatically adds a .WPD extension, so you don't need to worry about it.

Protecting a Document with a Password

If your document contains important information, you can protect it from snoops by assigning it a password. If anyone tries to open the file, they'll have to enter the correct password. To assign a password when you're saving a new document, follow these steps:

1. In the Save As dialog box, activate the Password Protect check box.

2. Select **OK** when you're ready to save the file. WordPerfect for Windows displays the Password dialog box (shown on the next page).

Use the Password dialog box to assign a password to sensitive documents.

3. In the Type Password for Document edit box, enter the password you want to use. WordPerfect for Windows displays the password in asterisks (just in case those darn snoops are looking over your shoulder).

4. Select **OK**. WordPerfect for Windows asks you to confirm your password.

5. Type your password again and then select **OK**.

If you forget your password, you're out of luck because there's no way to retrieve it. To prevent this, try to keep your passwords relatively short (5 or 6 letters) and meaningful.

To add a password to a document in version 5.2, select Password from the File menu, enter the password, select Set, re-enter the password to confirm, and then select Set again.

Saving a Document Under a New Name

The File menu also includes a Save As command. This command is a lot like Save, except that you can save the file to a new name or a new location. This is useful for creating a new file that is very similar (but not identical) to an existing file. Instead of creating the new file from scratch, just open the existing file, make the changes, and then use the Save As command (or press **F3**) to save your changes to the new file. The old file remains as it was.

This is also useful for adding a password to an existing file or removing a previously assigned password. Just open the file and select Save As from the File menu. In the Save As dialog box, activate or deactivate the Password Protect check box (whichever is appropriate), and then select **OK** (don't change the name of the file). When WordPerfect for Windows asks if you want to replace the file, select Yes. If you're adding password protection, you'll have to enter a password as described in the previous section.

Opening a Document

Each time you start WordPerfect for Windows, you see a blank typing area waiting patiently for you to type something. Most of the time, though, you'll want to work with an existing document you've saved sometime in the past. To do this, you need to tell WordPerfect for Windows to grab the appropriate file from wherever it's stored on disk, and *open* it in your computer's memory.

> To remove a password in WordPerfect for Windows 5.2, select Password from the **File** menu and select **Remove.**

To open a document, pull down the File menu and select the **Open** command, or press **Ctrl+O** (version 5.2 users press **F4**). You'll see the Open File dialog box shown here.

Open

Click on this tool in the Power Bar to display the Open File dialog box.

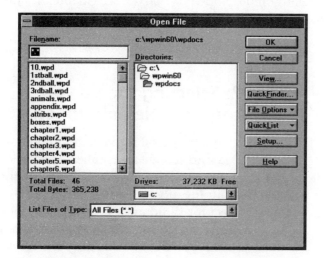

Selecting the Open command from the File menu displays the Open File dialog box.

The purpose of the Open File dialog box is to give you a reasonably coherent view of the files on your hard disk. The idea is that you browse through the files and then select the one you want to open. You'll be seeing this dialog box (or a variation of it) more often than you want to know, so let's take a closer look at just how you go about selecting a file.

Apartment Hunting Made Easy

To make this process of searching for a file a little more comprehensible, let's set up a simple analogy: the apartment search. When you're looking for an apartment, you first decide what city you want to live in. Once you know that, you can narrow your search to a specific area of the city. Finally, you narrow your search even further by deciding what type of apartment you want (bachelor, 1-bedroom, etc.). When all this is done, you end up with a short list of possible apartments, and you select the one you want from this list. Okay, let's put this analogy to work.

Step 1: Selecting the Correct Drive (the City)

Files can be stored on your hard disk or on floppy disks, so the first step is to make sure that you're dealing with the right drive. In our apartment hunting analogy, this is like selecting a city in which to live. The Drives drop-down list box displays the current drive, and you can use it to select a different drive, if necessary.

For all the gory details on drop-down list boxes, see Chapter 6, "Talking to WordPerfect for Windows' Dialog Boxes."

If you're going to select a floppy drive from the Drives list, make sure there's a disk in the drive. Otherwise, your computer will make a rude noise (on my system it sounds like somebody burping!) and will post a nasty message on the screen telling you, basically, to get your act together.

Step 2: Selecting the Correct Directory (the Neighborhood)

Just as cities are divided into neighborhoods, disks are divided into storage areas called *directories*. Use the Directories list box to select the correct directory for your file. If you're using version 6, WordPerfect for Windows sets up a default directory called WPDOCS for storing your WordPerfect documents. If you use this directory when saving your files, then you probably won't need to select a different directory.

If you forget how to select items from a list box, see Chapter 6, "Talking to WordPerfect for Windows' Dialog Boxes."

Step 3: Displaying the Proper File Type (the Type of Apartment)

There are many kinds of apartments and there are many kinds of files. And although a directory may contain dozens or even hundreds of files, there are only a few that you really need to look at. Use the List Files of Type drop-down list box to narrow the number of files displayed. WordPerfect for Windows 6 uses the WPD extension to identify its files, and those are the ones displayed in the Open File dialog box. If you've been saving your files with a different extension, you'll need to select the appropriate type from this drop-down list box.

Step 4: Selecting a File (the Apartment)

Now you're ready to make your selection. You've narrowed your search and the finalists are displayed in the Filename list box. Double-click on the file you want to open or highlight it and then select **OK**.

By the Way . . .

If you're not sure that a file is the one you want, highlight it and select the View button. WordPerfect for Windows displays the document in a Viewer window. To view other documents, just click on them in the Open File dialog box while the Viewer window is still open. When you see the one you want, select **OK**.

Opening Recent Files

If you want to reopen a document you worked with recently, you may not have to go through all this Open command rigmarole. Just pull down the File menu and look at the bottom. The names you see below the Exit command are the last four files you used. If one of them is the document you want, you're in luck! Just select it from the menu and WordPerfect will open it for you automatically.

Retrieving a File

When you retrieve a document, WordPerfect for Windows adds it to the current file at the insertion point position. This is a handy way of reusing material in another document.

When you want to retrieve a file, first position the insertion point where you want the new text to appear. Then select the File command from the Insert menu to display the Insert File dialog box. Highlight the document you want and then select the Insert button.

You retrieve a document in version 5.2 by selecting the **Retrieve** command from the **File** menu, highlighting the file in the Retrieve File dialog box, and then selecting **Retrieve**.

A Fresh Beginning: Starting a New Document

As I mentioned earlier, WordPerfect for Windows displays a new document when you start the program. However, you can start a fresh file anytime you want. All you do is pull down the File menu and select the **New** command, or press **Ctrl+N** (**Shift+F4** in version 5.2).

Click on this tool in the Power Bar to open a new document.

 New

Text that you use repeatedly is called *boilerplate*. It's the word processing equivalent of the old maxim, "Don't reinvent the wheel."

Closing a Document

When you're done with a document, you should close it to make room for other files. All you do is pull down the File menu and select the Close command, or press **Ctrl+F4**.

The Least You Need to Know

Now that was a chapter! WordPerfect for Windows sure seems to like complicating simple tasks such as saving and opening documents. Here's a summary of what you need to know:

☛ You should save your documents as often as you can to avoid losing any work. All you have to do is select the **S**ave command from the **F**ile menu (or press **Ctrl+S**).

☛ When saving a new document, WordPerfect for Windows will ask you to enter a name for the file. Be sure to follow DOS's arcane file-naming rules or you'll get an error.

☛ If you want to save a document under a different name, use the **F**ile menu's Save **A**s command (or press **F3**).

☛ To open a document, select **O**pen from the **F**ile menu (or press **Ctrl+O**), and select the file from the Open File dialog box.

☛ To retrieve a file, select the **I**nsert menu's **F**ile command.

☛ To close a document, use the **F**ile menu's **C**lose command (or press **Ctrl+F4**).

This page unintentionally left blank.

Chapter 8

Day-to-Day Drudgery II: Navigating Documents

In This Chapter

- ☛ Navigating a document with the keyboard
- ☛ Using WordPerfect for Windows' Go To command
- ☛ Navigating a document with a mouse
- ☛ Using scroll bars
- ☛ Tales of a thousand-and-one key combos

A lot of what you do in WordPerfect for Windows will be short little letters and memos that'll fit right on screen. But you'll also be creating longer documents, and what you see in the typing area will only be a small chunk of the entire file. To see the rest of the document, you'll need to learn a few *navigational* skills. Now, I'm not talking about navigating the Baja 500 or anything, but just a few simple skills to help you get around. With this chapter riding shotgun, you'll get through just fine.

By the Way . . .

To get the most out of this chapter, you should follow along and try each of the techniques as I present them. For best results, open (or create) a document that's larger than the screen.

TECHNO NERD TEACHES

When you hold down an arrow key, the speed at which the insertion point moves is governed by two factors: the *delay* after the first movement and the *repeat rate* (the rate at which the keyboard repeats the key). For the fastest possible keyboard (i.e., the shortest delay and the quickest repeat rate), try this: the next time you're in Program Manager, start the Control Panel (it should be in the Main group) and select the Keyboard icon. In the Keyboard dialog box, drag the boxes in both slider bars as far to the right as they'll go. Select **OK** and then exit Control Panel (by selecting Exit from the **S**ettings menu). Now start WordPerfect, and your insertion point keys will whizz around the screen.

SPEAK LIKE A GEEK

Moving text up or down is called *scrolling* through the document.

Navigating with the Keyboard

WordPerfect for Windows has a fistful of ways to navigate your documents from the keyboard. In this section, we'll work our way up from short hops between characters and words to great leaps between screens and pages.

Navigating Characters and Words

The simplest move you can make in a document is to use the left and right arrow keys to move left or right one character at a time. If you've got a bit of ground to cover, try holding down the key. After a slight delay, the insertion point will start racing through each line. (Notice that when it hits the end of one line, it starts over at the beginning of the next.)

If you need to jump over a couple of words, hold down the **Ctrl** key and then use the left or right arrow key to move one word at a time.

Navigating Lines and Paragraphs

If you need to move up or down one line at a time, use the up or down arrow key. If you're at the bottom of the screen and you press the down arrow, the text will move up so you can see the next line. (The line that used to be at the top of the screen heads off into oblivion, but don't worry: WordPerfect for Windows keeps track of everything.) A similar thing happens if you're at the top of the screen (unless you're at the top of the document): if you press the up arrow, the text moves down to make room for the next line.

To move to the beginning of the current line, press **Home**. To move to the end of the current line, press **End**.

If you need to jump around one paragraph at a time, use **Ctrl+up arrow** (to move up one paragraph) or **Ctrl+down arrow** (to move down one paragraph).

Navigating Screens, Pages, and Documents

For really big documents, you need to know how to cover a lot of ground in a hurry. WordPerfect for Windows, of course, is up to the task.

To move to the top of the screen, press **Page Up**. To move to the bottom of the screen, press **Page Down**. Keep pressing these keys to navigate the document one screenful at a time.

For multipage documents, use **Alt+Page Up** to move to the beginning of the previous page and **Alt+Page Down** to move to the beginning of the next page.

By the Way . . .

Once you start hopping madly through a file, get your bearings by keeping your eyes on the status bar's data. The Pg setting will tell you which page you're on, and the Ln setting tells you where you are on the current page.

For truly large leaps, press **Ctrl+Home** to move to the beginning of the document, or **Ctrl+End** to move to the end of the document.

Working with Bookmarks

When they stop reading a book, most people insert a bookmark of some kind (a piece of paper, the phone bill, the cat's tail, whatever) so they know where they left off. You can apply the same idea to your WordPerfect for Windows documents (if you're using version 6, that is). You can mark special points in your documents with the electronic equivalent of a bookmark, which lets you leap to those points quickly.

Creating a Bookmark

To create a bookmark, follow these steps:

1. Position the insertion point where you want to insert a bookmark.

2. Pull down the Insert menu and select the Bookmark command. The Bookmark dialog box appears.

3. Select the Create button. WordPerfect for Windows displays the Create Bookmark dialog box.

4. The Bookmark Name edit box will usually show a few words from the document. You can accept this or enter your own name, as shown below.

Use the Create Bookmark dialog box to identify your bookmark.

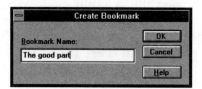

5. Select **OK** to return to the document.

6. Repeat steps 1–5 for any other bookmarks you want to insert.

Finding a Bookmark

Once you've defined your bookmarks, you can use them to jump giddily through your document. All you have to do is select Bookmark from the Insert menu again, highlight the bookmark you want from the Bookmark List, and then select the Go To button. WordPerfect for Windows leaps immediately to the marked spot.

Using the QuickMark Feature

If you have a favorite spot in a document, you can label it with a special bookmark called a QuickMark. Just position the insertion point on the spot and press **Ctrl+Shift+Q**. (If, for some reason, you want to do it the hard way, you can also choose Bookmark from the Insert menu and select the Set QuickMark button.)

To find the QuickMark, just press **Ctrl+Q**. Now *that's* quick! (Just for the record, the non-quick method is to choose Bookmark from the Insert menu, and select Find QuickMark.)

> ## By the Way . . .
> One of the best uses for a QuickMark is to mark your current position before you go traipsing off to another part of the document. If you set up a QuickMark before you go, you just have to press **Ctrl+Q** to return to where you were.

Navigating with the Go To Command

No document jockey's arsenal of navigation tricks would be complete without WordPerfect for Windows' Go To command. If you select Go To from the Edit menu, or press **Ctrl+G**, you'll see the Go To dialog box shown here.

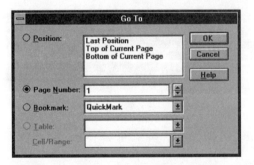

Use the Go To command to jump strategically through a document.

Go To lets you jump to specific parts of a document at warp speed. Here's a summary of some of the things you can do once the Go To dialog box is displayed:

Position   This option lets you choose either Last Position (where you were before you made your last leap), Top of Current Page, or Bottom of Current Page.

Page Number   This option lets you move to a specific page.
                    Type the number or use the spinner controls.

Bookmark   If you created any bookmarks, select one from
                    the drop-down list box.

How the Repeat Command Works

You can use the Repeat command to save some legwork. The idea is that
you enter a repeat number (8 is the default), then press a navigation key
combination (such as **Alt+Page Down**). WordPerfect for Windows will
then repeat the action the number of times you specified.

To try it out, select Repeat from the Edit menu to display the Repeat
dialog box (shown below). Enter the repeat number in the **Number of
Times to Repeat** spinner, and then select **OK**. Now just press the key
combination you want to repeat. If you leave the repeat number at 8 and
you press, say, Page Down, WordPerfect for Windows scrolls down 8
screens.

Use the Repeat dialog box to specify how many times Word-Perfect for Windows should repeat a key combination.

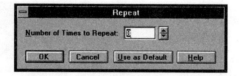

By the Way . . .

If you'd like to see another number besides 8 in the Repeat
dialog box, enter the number and then select the **Use** as
Default button. WordPerfect for Windows will use the new
number from now on.

Navigating a File with the Mouse

Keyboard users, of course, can't have *all* the fun. If you like using a mouse, you can still navigate a document. The most basic technique is simply to click on any visible part of the typing area and WordPerfect for Windows will move the insertion point to that position. This doesn't do you much good for long documents, however. No, to really get around with a mouse, you have to learn about scroll bars (see below).

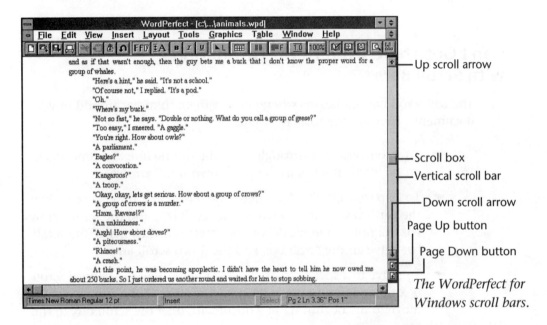

The WordPerfect for Windows scroll bars.

Scroll Whats?

Scroll bars are a lot like elevators. They sort of look like elevator shafts and, like your favorite Otis device, they serve a dual purpose: they can tell you where you are, and they can take you somewhere else.

Where Am I? The Scroll Bar Knows

Thanks to my innately lousy sense of direction, I always seem to get lost in any document longer than a couple of pages. Fortunately, I have scroll bars to bail me out. The idea is simple: the position of the scroll box in the vertical scroll bar tells me my relative position in the document. So, for example, if the scroll box is about halfway down, I know I'm somewhere near the middle of the file. They're just like the floor indicators on an elevator.

Can I Get There from Here? Navigating with Scroll Bars

The real scroll bar fun begins when you use them to move around in your documents. Here are the basic techniques:

- ☛ To scroll vertically through a document one line at a time, click on the vertical scroll bar's up or down scroll arrows.

- ☛ To leap through the document one screen at a time, click inside the vertical scroll bar between the scroll box and the scroll arrows. For example, to move down one screenful, click inside the scroll bar between the scroll box and the down scroll arrow.

- ☛ To move to a specific part of a document, drag the vertical scroll box up or down to the appropriate position. For example, to move to the beginning of a document, drag the scroll box to the top.

- ☛ To scroll to the top of the next page, click on the Page Down button.

- ☛ To scroll to the top of the previous page, click on the Page Up button.

The Least You Need to Know

This chapter concluded our look at document drudgery by examining a few easy navigation techniques. Here's the lowdown:

☛ Use the left and right arrow keys to move left and right one character at a time.

☛ Use **Ctrl+left arrow** or **Ctrl+right arrow** to jump left or right one word at a time.

☛ The up arrow and down arrow keys move you up or down one line at a time.

☛ Pressing **Ctrl+up arrow** moves you up one paragraph and **Ctrl+down arrow** moves you down one paragraph.

☛ Page Up moves you up one screen, while Page Down moves you down one screen.

☛ You can set up bookmarks to mark important places in your documents.

☛ When navigating with a mouse, just click to move to a spot you can see, or use the scroll bars to navigate the entire document.

This page unintentionally left blank.

Part II
Getting It Right: Editing Stuff

If, as they say, the essence of good writing is rewriting, then word processors ought to make us all better writers because rewriting—or editing—is what they do best. WordPerfect for Windows, in particular, has an impressive array of editing tools (some might say too impressive). The chapters in this section give you the basics of editing your prose in WordPerfect for Windows. You'll learn everything from simple deleting (and, thankfully, undeleting) to shuffling great hunks of text to new locations. I don't know if all this will make you a better writer, but it will sure make you a heck of a rewriter.

Chapter 9
Deleting Text (and Undeleting It, Too)

In This Chapter

- ☞ Deleting one character at a time
- ☞ Deleting one word at a time
- ☞ Deleting entire pages
- ☞ Using the Repeat and Undelete features
- ☞ A small slice of the author's life

I moved recently, and it only took me five minutes of packing to realize something: I'm a hoarder. (I said hoar*der*!) I never throw anything away: old gum wrappers; ticket stubs from every baseball, football, hockey, and basketball game I've ever attended; an ancient (and British!?) version of Monopoly. And books! Don't get me started with books!

I have the same trouble throwing things away when I'm writing. As my editor will tell you, I have a hard time deleting *anything*. (I think I just get too attached.) However, that's not WordPerfect for Windows' fault, because it gives you all kinds of ways to nix troublesome text. This chapter will show you how.

Before going on any kind of deletion rampage, you should know that there's a section at the end of this chapter called "To Err Is Human, to Undelete Divine." If you wipe out anything you shouldn't have, read ahead to this section to see how to make everything okay again.

In *Typeover mode*, your typing replaces existing characters. With *Insert mode*, your typing is inserted between existing characters.

Deleting Characters

Did you spell *potato* with an *e* again? (Perhaps you have political aspirations.) Or perhaps you've just seen the Queen on TV, and have been using words like *colour* and *cheque*. Well, not to worry; WordPerfect for Windows makes it easy to expunge individual characters. You have two options:

- ☞ Press the **Delete** key to delete the character to the right of the insertion point.

- ☞ Press **Backspace** to delete the character to the left of the insertion point.

If you'd like to delete several characters in a row, hold down **Delete** or **Backspace** until all the riffraff is eliminated. (Be careful, though: the insertion point really picks up speed if you hold it down for more than a second or two.) You can also switch to Typeover mode (by pressing **Insert**), and simply overwrite the text you want deleted. Just remember to return to Insert mode when you're done (by pressing **Insert** again).

Deleting Words

To handle any stray words that creep into your documents, WordPerfect for Windows lets you delete entire words with a single stroke. Just position the insertion point anywhere inside the word you want to blow away, and press **Ctrl+Backspace**.

By the Way . . .

If you place the insertion point between two words and press Ctrl+Backspace, WordPerfect for Windows deletes the word to the left of the insertion point.

Deleting Lines

WordPerfect for Windows lets you delete a portion of a line, or even (with just a little extra work) an entire line. For starters, if you just need to delete text from the insertion point to the end of the line, press **Ctrl+Delete**.

Deleting an entire line takes an extra step: first place the insertion point at the beginning of the line (by pressing **Home** or by clicking to the left of the line) and *then* press **Ctrl+Delete**.

> ## By the Way . . .
>
> To learn how to delete entire sentences and paragraphs, see Chapter 10, "Block Partying: Working with Blocks of Text."

Deleting Pages

If you've really made a mess of things, you may need to obliterate great chunks of text. One handy way to do this is to delete everything from the insertion point to the end of the page. You do this by pressing **Ctrl+Shift+Delete**.

> ## By the Way . . .
>
> Recall that WordPerfect for Windows places a line across the screen to show you where one page ends and another begins. To be safe, you should scroll down to the bottom of the page before using **Ctrl+Shift+Delete** to make sure you're not going to wipe out anything important.

Repeat Deleting

The Repeat command is a handy way to speed up your deletion chores. Just select Repeat from the Edit menu, enter the number of repetitions you want, and then select **OK**. Now press the appropriate deletion key or key combination, and WordPerfect for Windows will repeat it the number of times you specified. For example, if you set the default repeat value at 8 and press **Ctrl+Backspace**, WordPerfect will delete the next eight words.

To Err Is Human, to Undelete Divine

Let's face facts: *everybody* deletes stuff accidentally, and one day *you'll* do it, too. It's one of those reality things (like nose hair and paying taxes) that we just can't avoid. The good people at WordPerfect know this, and the gurus in their programming department came up with a way to ease the pain: the Undelete command. This command, as its name implies, miraculously reverses any of your three most recent deletions. (Which, believe me, has saved *my* bacon on more than one occasion.)

Here are the steps to follow to undelete something:

1. Get whatever cursing, fuming, and gesticulating you normally do when you've just deleted your last three hours work out of the way first. You need a clear head for what's to come.

2. Select Undelete from the Edit menu, or press **Ctrl+Shift+Z** (**Alt+Shift+Backspace** in version 5.2). As you can see on the next page, WordPerfect for Windows displays the Undelete dialog box, adds the last deletion back into the text, and highlights it so you can see it clearly.

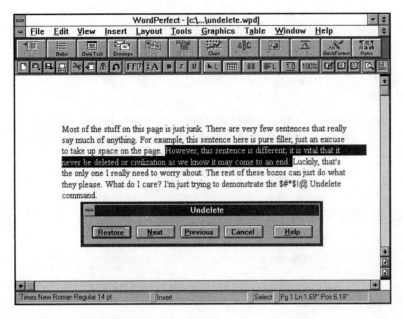

Most of the stuff on this page is just junk. There are very few sentences that really say much of anything. For example, this sentence here is pure filler, just an excuse to take up space on the page. However, this sentence is different; it is vital that it never be deleted or civilization as we know it may come to an end. Luckily, that's the only one I really need to worry about. The rest of these bozos can just do what they please. What do I care? I'm just trying to demonstrate the $#*$!@ Undelete command.

When you select the Undelete command, WordPerfect for Windows adds the last deletion back into the text, and displays the Undelete dialog box.

3. If that's the text you want undeleted, select **Restore**. If it's not, select **Previous** deletion until you see what you want, and then select **Restore**. (Remember that WordPerfect for Windows only stores the last three things you deleted.)

TECHNO NERD TEACHES

How does Undelete perform its magic? Well, each time you delete something, it might appear as though it has gone off to some la-la land of deleted text, but that's not quite the case. WordPerfect for Windows sneakily saves each of the last three deletions in a special file called a *buffer* that stores not only the text itself, but its original location as well. Undeleting, then, is a simple matter of restoring the text from the buffer.

The Least You Need to Know

This compact little chapter gave you the scoop on deleting text (and undeleting it too, just in case). Here are a few pointers to take with you on your travels:

☞ To delete individual characters, use the **Delete** key (to delete whatever is to the right of the insertion point), or the **Backspace** key (to delete whatever is to the left of the insertion point).

☞ To delete a word, put the insertion point inside the word and press **Ctrl+Backspace**.

☞ Press **Ctrl+Delete** to delete from the current insertion point position to the end of the line.

☞ To delete from the current insertion point position to the end of the page, press **Ctrl+Shift+Delete**.

☞ You can speed up your deleting by using the Repeat command. Just pull down the Edit menu and select the Repeat command to display the Repeat dialog box. Enter a different number, if needed, select **OK** to return to the document, and then press the appropriate deletion key or key combo.

☞ If you delete something by accident, immediately select **U**ndelete from the **E**dit menu (or press **Ctrl+Shift+Z**). Select **R**estore to undelete the highlighted text, or select **P**revious to see other deleted text.

Chapter 10

Block Partying: Working with Blocks of Text

In This Chapter

- ☛ How to select a block of text
- ☛ Making copies of text blocks
- ☛ Moving text blocks to different locations within a document
- ☛ Reversing errors with the Undo command
- ☛ Pleasurable prose chock-a-block with practical WordPerfect for Windows stuff

Blocs (as in the "Eastern bloc") may be out, but *blocks* are definitely in. I mean, we have block parents, block parties, block captains. Why even the old *Gumby and Pokey* show (which featured the villainous Blockheads, of course) has made a bizarre comeback of sorts.

WordPerfect for Windows uses blocks, too. In this case, though, a *block* is just a section of text. It could be a word, a sentence, two-and-half paragraphs, or 57 pages—whatever you need. The key is that WordPerfect for Windows treats a block as a single entity: a unit. And what does one do with these units? Well, you name it; they can be copied, moved, deleted, printed, formatted, spell-checked, taken to lunch, whatever. This chapter not only shows you how to select a block, but it also takes you through a few of these block tasks.

A *block* is a section of text of any length.

Selecting a Block of Text

WordPerfect for Windows, bless its electronic heart, gives you no less than three ways to select a block of text: you can use your keyboard, your mouse, or the handy Select command.

Selecting Text with the Keyboard

To select some text with your keyboard, begin by positioning the insertion point at the beginning of the text. Now hold down the **Shift** key and use the arrow keys to move through the text you want to select. As you do, the characters you're selecting become highlighted (i.e., they appear white on a black background), as you can see here. If you decide you don't want to select the text after all, just press **Esc**.

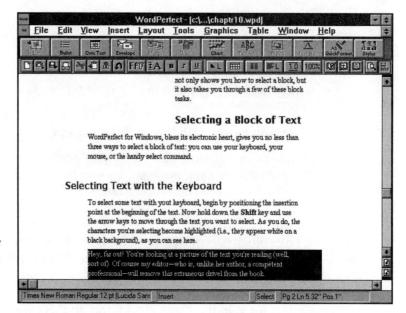

When you select text, WordPerfect for Windows displays the highlighted characters as white text on a black background.

For more fine-tuned selecting, Table 10.1 presents some key combos you can use to select text.

Table 10.1   Key Combinations to Use While Selecting Text

Press	To Select Text to
Ctrl+Shift+right arrow	The next word
Ctrl+Shift+left arrow	The previous word
Shift+End	The end of the line
Shift+Home	The beginning of the line
Ctrl+Shift+down arrow	The end of the paragraph
Ctrl+Shift+up arrow	The beginning of the paragraph
Shift+Page Down	The bottom of the screen
Shift+Page Up	The top of the screen
Ctrl+Shift+End	The bottom of the document
Ctrl+Shift+Home	The top of the document

By the Way . . .

The sharp-eyed will have noticed that the key combinations in Table 10.1 bear a remarkable resemblance to the navigation keys you struggled through back in Chapter 8. Hey, you get an extra dessert tonight—because, yes, they're exactly the same! The only difference is that you hold down the Shift key to get the "Select" feature. In fact, you can use any of the stuff from that chapter (including the handy **G**o To command) to select text.

Selecting Text with the Mouse

Mouse users, forget the keyboard; selecting text with the little rodent guy is *way* easier. All you have to do is position the pointer at the beginning of the block, press and hold down the left button, and then drag the mouse over the text you want to select. That's it! No unsightly key combinations! And if you have a lot of text to select, just click at the beginning of the text, hold down **Shift**, and then click at the end of the text. WordPerfect for Windows will automatically select everything in between.

But wait, there's more! You can use the mouse techniques in Table 10.2 for even more block fun.

Table 10.2   Mouse Techniques for Selecting Text

Do This	To Select
Double-click on a word	The word
Click in the left margin	A sentence
Double-click in the left margin	A paragraph
Triple-click inside a sentence	The sentence
Quadruple-click inside a paragraph	The paragraph

Using the Select Command

WordPerfect for Windows' Select command makes it easy to select single sentences, paragraphs, or even the entire document. Just position the insertion point in the appropriate sentence or paragraph (if that's what you want to select), and then run the Edit menu's Select command. You'll see a cascade menu appear with several options, four of which we care about here:

Sentence   Selects the current sentence.

Paragraph   Selects the current paragraph.

Page   Selects the current page.

All   Selects the entire document.

If you have a mouse and WordPerfect for Windows version 6, you can take advantage of the right mouse button to select a sentence, paragraph, or document easily. Just right-click in the left margin to display the

QuickMenu shown below. Then simply click on Select Sentence to select the current sentence, Select Paragraph to select the current paragraph, Select Page to select the current page, and Select All to select—you guessed it—the entire document.

```
Select Sentence
Select Paragraph
Select Page
Select All

Margins...
Outline...

Comment...
Sound...
Subdocument...
```

One of WordPerfect for Windows' QuickMenus (version 6 only).

Selecting Text with Bookmarks

Bookmarks (as you saw in Chapter 8) provide a handy way to navigate a document. But you can also use them to mark blocks so you can reselect them quickly. Follow these steps to check this out (remember: you need version 6 to use bookmarks):

1. Select the block you want to mark.

2. Select the Insert menu's Bookmark command and, when the Bookmark dialog box appears, select the Create button.

3. Enter a name for the selection and then select OK.

4. To reselect the block later on, select the Bookmark command again, highlight the bookmark in the Bookmark List, and then select the Go To & Select button. WordPerfect for Windows obligingly reselects the entire block.

> ### By the Way . . .
>
> As if all this wasn't enough, you can also use the **Go To** command to select—or, in this case, reselect—text (provided you're using version 6). Just select **Go To** from the **Edit** menu (or press **Ctrl+G**), and in the **Position** list, select **Reselect Last Selection**. Select **OK** and WordPerfect for Windows will return you to the document with the last block selected.

Copying a Block

One of the secrets of computer productivity is a simple maxim: "Don't reinvent the wheel." In other words, if you've got something that works, and you need something similar, don't start from scratch. Instead, make a copy of the original, and then make whatever changes are necessary to the copy.

Happily, WordPerfect for Windows makes it easy to copy stuff. In fact, you get two methods: the Copy command and something called "drag-and-drop."

Using the Copy Command

Once you've selected the block you want to copy, all you have to do is pull down the Edit menu and select the Copy command, or press **Ctrl+C** (in version 5.2, press **Ctrl+Insert**). You then position the insertion point where you want to place the copy and select **Paste** from the Edit menu, or press **Ctrl+V** (**Shift+Insert** in 5.2). A perfect copy of your selection appears instantly. If you need to make other copies, position the insertion point appropriately, and select the **Paste** command again.

Click on this tool in version 6's Power Bar to copy a block.

Copy

Click on this tool in the Power Bar to paste a block.

Paste

By the Way . . .

You can also use the QuickMenus for your copying chores. When you've selected the block, right-click anywhere inside the page and then select Copy from the QuickMenu. Now position the insertion point where you want the copy to go, right-click again, and this time select Paste from the QuickMenu.

Copying with Drag-and-Drop

WordPerfect for Windows' *drag-and-drop* technique is one of my favorite features. The idea is that you use your mouse to physically drag a copy of a block from one part of a document to another. Here's what you do:

1. Select the block you want to copy.

2. Position the mouse pointer anywhere inside the block, hold down the **Ctrl** key, and then press and hold down the left mouse button. The mouse pointer should now look like this:

3. Move the mouse to where you want the copy to appear (this is the "dragging" part).

4. Release the mouse button (this is the "dropping" part), and then release **Ctrl**. WordPerfect for Windows copies the block, as pretty as you please.

Moving a Block

One of the all-time handiest word processor features is the ability to move stuff from one part of a document to another. This is perfect for rearranging everything from single sentences to humongous chunks of text.

Now, you might think you'd do this by making a copy, pasting it, and then going back and deleting the original. Well, you *could* do it that way, but your friends would almost certainly laugh at you. Why? Because there's an easier way. WordPerfect for Windows lets you *cut* a selection right out of a document, and then paste it somewhere else. And version 6 gives you (as with copying) two methods.

Moving with the Cut Command

Once you've selected what you want to move, pull down the Edit menu and select the Cut command, or press **Ctrl+X**. (Version 5.2 types press **Shift+Del**.) Your selection will disappear from the screen, but don't panic:

WordPerfect for Windows is saving it for you in a secret location. Now position the insertion point where you want to move the selection and choose Paste from the Edit menu. Your stuff miraculously reappears in the new location. If you need to make further copies of the selection, just reposition the insertion point and select Paste again.

Click on this tool in the Power Bar to cut a block.

Cut

> ## By the Way . . .
> Yes, you can use the QuickMenus for moving. With a block selected, right-click anywhere inside the page and then select Cut from the QuickMenu. Position the insertion point where you want to move the text, right-click again, and select **Paste** from the QuickMenu.

If you cut a selection accidentally, immediately select Undo from the Edit menu, or press **Ctrl+Z** (use **Alt+Backspace** in 5.2). For more Undo info, see the section titled "The Life-Saving Undo Command" later in this chapter.

Moving with Drag-and-Drop

Yes, our old friend drag-and-drop can move text, too. This is very similar to copying as you see here:

1. Select the block you want to move.

2. Position the mouse pointer anywhere inside the block and then press and hold down the left mouse button. The mouse pointer will change into this:

3. Drag the mouse to where you want to move the text.

4. Release the mouse button. WordPerfect for Windows moves your text to the new location.

Saving a Block

If you've just written a block of some particularly breathtaking prose, you might want to save it in a file all its own. No sweat. Just select it, pull down the File menu, and choose the Save command. WordPerfect for Windows displays the Save dialog box, shown below. Make sure the Selected Text option is activated and then select **OK**. You'll see the Save As dialog box on-screen. Just enter the information as though you were saving a file. (See Chapter 7, "Day-to-Day Drudgery I: Opening, Saving, and Closing," for details.) Enter a name for the file in the **Filename** edit box, and then select **OK**.

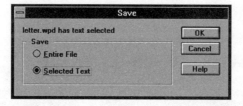

Use the Save dialog box to save a high-lighted block to a file.

Deleting a Block

Deleting a block of text is a no-brainer. Just make your selection, and then press either **Delete** or **Backspace**. Remember that if you delete anything accidentally, you can always fall back on WordPerfect for Windows' Undelete command. See Chapter 9, "Deleting Text (and Undeleting It, Too)," for the skinny on Undelete.

By the Way . . .

Mouse mavens can delete stuff quickly, too. Simply select the block you want to blow away, right-click inside the page, and then select **Delete** from the QuickMenu that appears.

> Make sure you select the **Undo** command *immediately* after making your mistake. WordPerfect for Windows can only reverse your last action, so if you do anything else in the meantime, you may not be able to recover.

The Life-Saving Undo Command

Every WordPerfect for Windows user—from the rawest novice to the nerdiest expert—ends up at some time or other doing something downright silly. It may be cutting when you should have been copying, or just pasting a chunk of text in some absurd location.

Fortunately, WordPerfect for Windows has an Undo feature to get you out of these jams. The Undo command restores everything to the way it was before you made your blunder. (I've had some relationships where an Undo command would have come in *real* handy.) All you have to do is pull down the Edit menu and select Undo, or press **Ctrl+Z** (**Alt+Backspace** in version 5.2).

The Least You Need to Know

This chapter led you through the basics of working with WordPerfect for Windows' text blocks. We really only scratched the surface here, because there's plenty more you can do with blocks. However, I'll save all that rot for the chapters to come. For now, here's a rehash of what just happened:

☞ A block is a selection of text that you can work with as a unit.

☞ To select text with the keyboard, hold down the **Shift** key and then use WordPerfect for Windows' navigation keys to highlight the text you want.

☞ Selecting text with a mouse is even easier. Position the pointer at the beginning of the text, and then drag the mouse over the selection you need.

- ☞ To copy a block, select **Copy** from the **Edit** menu, position the insertion point, and select **Paste**. Alternatively, hold down **Ctrl** and use your mouse to drag a copy of the block to the new location.

- ☞ To move a block, pull down the **Edit** menu and select **Cut**, position the insertion point, and then select **Paste** from the **Edit** menu. You can also simply drag the block to its new locale with your mouse.

- ☞ To delete a block, just press **Delete** or **Backspace**.

- ☞ To reverse a blunder, immediately select **Undo** from the **Edit** menu.

This page unintentionally left blank.

Chapter 11
Search and Ye Shall Replace

In This Chapter

- ☞ Searching for text, forwards
- ☞ Searching for text, backwards
- ☞ Search strategies
- ☞ Searching for and replacing text
- ☞ A sad little song, sure to bring a tear to your eye

Oh where, oh where has my little text gone?
Oh where, oh where can it be?

If you've ever found yourself lamenting a long-lost word adrift in some humongous megadocument, the folks at WordPerfect for Windows can sympathize (probably because it has happened to *them* a time or two). In fact, they were even kind enough to build a special Find feature into WordPerfect for Windows to help you search for missing text. And that's not all: you can also use the related Replace feature to seek out and *replace* every instance of one word with another. Sound like fun? Well, okay, but it *is* handy, so you might want to read this chapter anyway.

Finding Text

If you need to find a certain word or phrase in a short document, it's usually easiest just to scroll through the text. But if you're dealing with more than a couple of pages, don't waste your time rummaging through the whole file. WordPerfect for Windows' Find feature lets you search forward (toward the end of the document) or backward (toward the beginning) to find what you need.

Searching Forwards

Here are the steps you need to follow to search for a piece of text from the current insertion point position to the end of the document:

1. Pull down the Edit menu and select the Find command, or press F2. The Find Text dialog box appears, as shown below.

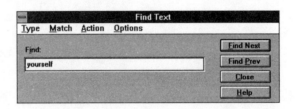

Use the Find Text dialog box to hunt for text in a document.

2. In the Find edit box, type the text you want to find.

3. Select the Find Next button. If WordPerfect for Windows finds a match, it selects it and displays it on the screen. If no match is found, WordPerfect for Windows displays a message to that effect (which you can remove from the screen by selecting **OK**). In both cases, you end up back in the Find Text dialog box.

4. Either repeat steps 2 and 3 to resume the search, or select the Close button to return to the document.

> In WordPerfect for Windows 5.2, select **Search** from the **Edit** menu (or press **F2**), and enter your text in the Search **For** edit box. Make sure the **Direction** pop-up says **Forward** and then select **Search**. To resume the search, select Search Next from the **Edit** menu, or press **Shift+F2**.

Searching Backwards

If you suspect the text you need to find is back toward the beginning of the document, you can tell WordPerfect for Windows to search *backwards*, instead. Here are the steps to follow:

1. Select Find from the Edit menu, or press **F2**.

2. Type your search text in the Find edit box.

3. Select the Find **Prev** button. If WordPerfect for Windows finds a match, it selects it and displays it. Otherwise, a message appears to tell you you're out of luck. (You remove it, again, by selecting **OK**.) WordPerfect for Windows returns you to the Find Text dialog box, in either case.

4. Repeat steps 2 and 3 to resume the search, or select the Close button to return to the document.

> **5.2**
>
> In WordPerfect for Windows 5.2, select **S**earch from the Edit menu (or press **F2**), enter your text in the Search For edit box, and select **Backward** in the Direction pop-up. Select **S**earch to get things started. To resume the search, select Search **P**revious from the Edit menu, or press **Alt+F2**.

Some Notes on Searching

Searching for text is a pretty straightforward affair, but it wouldn't be WordPerfect for Windows if there weren't five thousand other ways to confuse the heck out of us. To make things easier, here are a few plain-English notes that'll help you get the most out of the Find feature:

☞ For best results, don't try to match entire sentences. A word or two is usually all you really need.

☞ If you're not sure how to spell a word, just use a piece of it. WordPerfect for Windows will still find *egregious* if you search for *egre* (although it'll also find words like *regret* and *degree*).

☛ To find only words that *begin* with your search text, add a space before the text.

☛ Rather than fumbling around with searching both forward and backward, WordPerfect for Windows gives you two commands on the **O**ptions menu in the Find Text dialog box. Activate the **B**egin Find At Top of Document command to always start searching from the top. Activate the **W**rap at Beg./End of Document command to force WordPerfect for Windows to continue searching at the top of the document once it has reached the bottom.

☛ If you need to differentiate between, say, *Bobby* (some guy) and *bobby* (as in a *bobby* pin or an English *bobby*), activate the **C**ase command from the **M**atch menu in the Find Text dialog box. This tells WordPerfect for Windows to match not only the letters, but also whatever uppercase and lowercase format you use.

☛ If you search for, say, *gorge*, WordPerfect for Windows may find not only the word *gorge*, but also *gorged*, *gorgeous*, and *disgorge* as well. If all you want is *gorge*, activate the **M**atch menu's **W**hole Word command.

Finding and Replacing Text

If you do a lot of writing, one of the features you'll come to rely on the most is *find and replace*. This means that WordPerfect for Windows seeks out a particular bit of text and then replaces it with something else. This may not seem like a big deal for a word or two, but if you need to change a couple of dozen instances of *irregardless* to *regardless*, it can be a real time-saver.

Find and Replace: The Basic Steps

Finding and replacing is, as you might imagine, not that different from plain old finding. Here's how it works:

1. Select the **R**eplace command from the **E**dit menu. You'll see the Find and Replace Text dialog box shown on the next page.

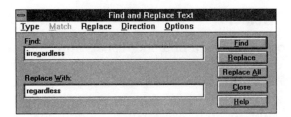

Use the Find and Replace Text dialog box to find text and then replace it with something else.

2. In the Find edit box, enter the text you want to find.

3. In the Replace With edit box, enter the text you want to use as a replacement.

4. If you're sure you want to replace every instance of the text in the Find box, select the Replace All button. If you'd like to verify the replacements, select Find, instead.

5. If you chose the Replace All button, WordPerfect for Windows merrily chugs along replacing everything in sight. When it's done, it displays a message to that effect. Select **OK** to return to the Find and Replace Text dialog.

    If you selected Find and WordPerfect for Windows finds a match, it highlights the text and displays it on-screen. Select **Replace** to confirm the replacement, or select Find to look for the next match. (You could also select Replace All to let WordPerfect go crazy.)

    If WordPerfect for Windows doesn't find a match, a message appears to tell you the bad news. Select **OK** to return to the dialog box.

6. Keep repeating step 5 until you're done. Select Close to return to the document.

By the Way . . .

To keep your find-and-replace operations focused, you can first select a block (glance back at Chapter 10, "Block Party-ing: Working with Text Blocks," if you need to learn block basics). This tells WordPerfect for Windows to find and replace *only* within the block.

Find and Replace Options

To get the most out of the powerful find-and-replace stuff, you'll probably want to test-drive a few options. Here's what's available in the Find and Replace dialog box:

☞ Use the Direction menu to select a direction for the search. You can activate either the Forward or Backward command.

☞ Many of the Find and Replace Text dialog box options are identical to those in the Find Text dialog box. In particular, you can perform case-sensitive searches, find whole words only, and force WordPerfect for Windows to search the entire document.

☞ Sometimes, you want to replace only the first few occurrences of a piece of text. In this case, select the Limit Number of Changes command from the Options menu and enter the number of replacements you want in the dialog box that appears.

☞ If you want to search and *delete* text, just leave the Replace With edit box blank and proceed normally (although, in this case, it's probably a good idea to avoid the Replace All button).

Put It to Work

Find and replace is one of those features for which you'll find endless uses. But perhaps one of the best is to weed out words used improperly. For example, you might need to replace some instances of *affect* with *effect* (one of my personal bugaboos). Here's a list of some of the most commonly confused words you might want to check for (in most cases you can reverse the *Find* and *Replace with* terms, depending on which usage is correct):

Find	Replace with
affect (to influence)	effect (a result)
already (action has happened)	all ready (entirely ready)
alright (no such word)	all right
all together (as one)	altogether (entirely)
any body (any human form)	anybody (any person)
averse (disinclined)	adverse (opposed)

Find	Replace with
breath (inhalation)	breathe (to inhale)
capitol (govt. building)	capital (seat of govt.)
censure (to blame)	censor (to expurgate)
continual (frequently recurring)	continuous (uninterrupted)
different than (improper)	different from
hanged (refers to a person)	hung (refers to an object)
irregardless (improper)	regardless
momento (wrong)	memento
regretful (improper)	regrettable
seasonable (timely)	seasonal (periodical)

The Least You Need to Know

This chapter introduced you to WordPerfect for Windows' handy **Find** and **Replace** features. Here's a fond look back:

- ☞ To search forward for some text, select **Find** from the **Edit** menu (or press **F2**), enter the search text, and then select the **Find** Next button.

- ☞ To search backward, select the **Edit** menu's **Find** command, enter the search text, and then select the Find **Prev** button.

- ☞ If you're searching for proper names and other things where case matters, make sure you activate the **Case** command from the **Match** menu.

- ☞ The Find and Replace feature is a great way to replace every instance of a word or phrase quickly. To use it, select **Replace** from the **Edit** menu (or press **Ctrl+F2**), enter your text in the Find and Replace **With** boxes, and then select **Find**, **Replace**, or Replace **All** button.

This page unintentionally left blank.

Part III
Looking Good: Formatting Stuff

"The least you can do is look respectable." That's what my mother always used to tell me when I was a kid. This advice holds up especially well in these image-conscious times. If you don't look good up front (or if your work doesn't look good), then you'll often be written off without a second thought.

When it comes to looking good—whether you're writing up a memo, slicking up a report, or polishing up your resume´ —WordPerfect for Windows gives you a veritable cornucopia of formatting options. The chapters in this part give you the skinny on these various options, including lots of hints about how best to use them.

Chapter 12
Making Your Characters Look Good

In This Chapter

- ☛ Applying character attributes such as bold and italics
- ☛ Using different character sizes
- ☛ Converting letters between uppercase and lowercase
- ☛ Working with different fonts
- ☛ Adding WordPerfect for Windows' symbols to your documents
- ☛ Frighteningly fun formatting frolics

The first step on our road to looking good is the lowly character. I know, I know, you want to try out some really *big* stuff, but don't forget all that blather about the longest journey beginning with a single step. Besides, working with characters *can* make a big difference. Why, just a little bit of bolding here, a couple of italics there, throw in a font or two, and suddenly that humdrum, boring memo is turned into a dynamic, exciting thing of beauty. People from all over will be clamoring to read your stuff. You will be, in short, a star.

Working with Fonts

Until now, you may not have given much thought to the individual characters that make up your writings. After all, an *a* is an *a*, isn't it? Well, WordPerfect for Windows will change all that. When you start working with different *fonts*, you'll see that not all *a*'s are the same (or *b*'s or *c*'s for that matter).

Just What the Heck Is a Font, Anyway?

Fonts are to characters what architecture is to buildings. In architecture, you look at certain features and patterns; if you can tell a geodesic dome from a flying buttress, you can tell whether the building is Gothic or Art Deco or whatever. Fonts, too, are distinguished by a set of unique design characteristics. Specifically, there are four things to look for: the typeface, the type style, the type size, and the type position.

The Typeface

Any related set of letters, numbers, and other symbols has its own distinctive design called the *typeface*. Typefaces, as you can see on the next page, can be wildly different depending on the shape and thickness of characters, the spacing, and what the designer had for breakfast that day.

Typefaces come in three flavors: *serif, sans-serif,* or *decorative.* A serif typeface contains fine cross strokes—typographic technoids call them *feet*—at the extremities of each character. These subtle appendages give the typeface a traditional, classy look. Times New Roman (shown on the next page) is a common example of a serif typeface.

A sans serif typeface doesn't contain these cross strokes. As a result, serif typefaces usually have a cleaner, more modern look (check out Arial in the picture).

Decorative typefaces are usually special designs used to convey a particular effect. So, for example, if your document really needs a Gothic atmosphere, Lucida Blackletter (shown on the next page) would be perfect.

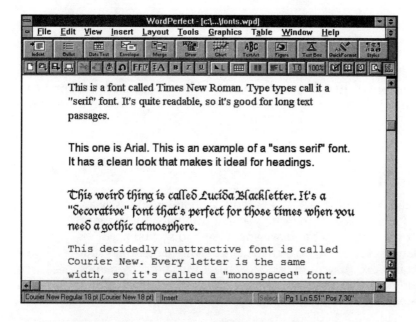

As these examples show, typefaces can be very different.

You can also classify typefaces according to the space they allot for each character. This is called the *character spacing* of a font, and it can take two forms: *monospaced* or *proportional*. Monospaced fonts reserve the same amount of space for each character. For example, look at the Courier New font shown earlier. Notice that skinny letters, such as "i" and "l," take up as much space as wider letters, such as "y" and "w." While this is admirably egalitarian, these fonts tend to look like they were produced with a typewriter (in other words, they're *ugly*). By contrast, in a proportional font such as Arial or Times New Roman, the space allotted to each letter varies according to the width of the letter.

The Type Style

The *type style* of a font usually refers to whether the characters are **bold** or *italic*. WordPerfect for Windows also lets you set character attributes like underlining and ~~strikeout~~ (sometimes called "strikethrough"). These styles are normally used to highlight or add emphasis to sections of your documents.

The Type Size

The *type size* just measures how tall a font is. The standard unit of measurement is the *point*, where there are 72 points in an inch. So, for example, the individual letters in a 24-point font would be twice as tall as those in a 12-point font. (In case you're wondering, this book is printed in a 10-point font.)

Put It to Work

Using different character sizes and attributes is an easy way to fool people into thinking you're a competent professional. For example, you can make your titles and section headings stand out by using bold characters that are larger than your regular text. Italics are good for things like company names and book titles, and you can also use them for emphasizing important words or phrases.

Technically, type size is measured from the highest point of a tall letter, such as "f," to the lowest point of an underhanging letter, such as "g."

The Type Position

Characters normally follow each other along each line, But you can also format the relative *position* of characters to get superscripts (slightly higher than normal) or subscripts (slightly lower than normal), as shown on the next page.

Selecting Different Fonts

Okay, enough theory. Let's get down to business and see how you go about selecting different fonts for your documents. To begin with, select the block of text you want to format (by holding down **Shift** and using the arrow keys or by dragging your mouse over the text; see Chapter 10, "Block Partying: Working with Blocks of Text," for details). You then need to display the Font dialog box using any one of the following three methods (depending on your mood):

☞ Pull down the Layout menu and select the Font command.

☞ Press **F9**.

☞ Right-click inside the typing area and select Font from the QuickMenu.

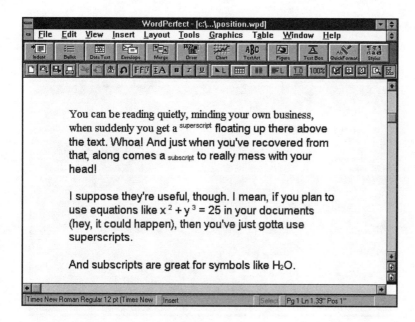

You can be reading quietly, minding your own business, when suddenly you get a superscript floating up there above the text. Whoa! And just when you've recovered from that, along comes a subscript to really mess with your head!

I suppose they're useful, though. I mean, if you plan to use equations like $x^2 + y^3 = 25$ in your documents (hey, it could happen), then you've just gotta use superscripts.

And subscripts are great for symbols like H_2O.

WordPerfect for Windows lets you change the relative position of characters to get superscripts and subscripts.

In each case, you'll see the Font dialog box shown on the next page.

From here, selecting the font you want is easy:

5.2

WordPerfect for Windows version 5.2 users need to select Font from the Font menu or press **F9**.

☞ Use the Font Face list to pick out a typeface.

☞ For the type style, you can either use the Font Style list or you can select individual attributes from the check boxes in the Appearance group.

☞ Use the Font Size list to select the type size. If you're not sure which point size you need, you can also use the Relative Size pop-up list to pick a size, such as Small or Very Large.

In version 5.2, you can also choose some character attributes right from the Font menu.

☛ Use the **Position** pop-up list to select either Normal, Subscript, or Superscript.

When you're done, select **OK** to return to the document.

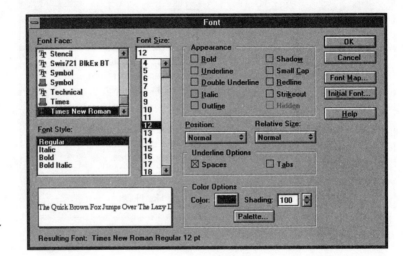

Use the Font dialog box for your character formatting chores.

By the Way . . .

When you make your selections in the Font dialog box, keep an eye peeled on the Resulting Font box. This will give you an idea of what your font will look like.

Click on this tool in the Power Bar to display a list of fonts.

 This Power Bar tool displays a list of font sizes.

 You can click on this tool in the Power Bar to apply the bold attribute.

 Click on this tool in the Power Bar to apply the italics attribute.

 This Power Bar tool applies the underline attribute.

Instead of changing existing text, you might prefer to have any *new* text you type appear in a certain font. This is even easier; just select the font options you want from the Font dialog box, select **OK**, and then start typing. WordPerfect for Windows displays subsequent characters in the font you chose.

You can also use the following shortcut keys for character formatting: **Ctrl+B** for bold, **Ctrl+I** for italics, and **Ctrl+U** for underline.

Working with Initial Fonts

Every document has what WordPerfect for Windows calls an *initial font*. This is just the default font that appears before you've selected any font options. If you want your regular text to appear in a different font, you can change the initial font to whatever you like (although you only get to choose a different typeface or type size, and your type styles are limited to bold and italic). Here's how it's done:

☞ To change the initial font for the current document, display the Font dialog box, select the Initial Font button, and then select your font from the Document Initial Font dialog box that appears. Select **OK** to return to the Font dialog, and then select **OK** again to return to your document with the new font in effect.

☛ To change the initial font for every new document you create, choose Select Printer from the File menu to display the Select Printer dialog box. Make sure the printer you normally use is highlighted in the Printers list and then select the Initial Font button. Use the Printer Initial Font dialog box to select your font and then select OK. Select Close to return to the document.

> ### By the Way . . .
> If you need more info about selecting different printers, see Chapter 16, "Getting It Down on Paper: Printing Documents."

To set an initial font for new documents in version 5.2, choose Select Printer from the File menu, select the Setup button from the Select Printer dialog box, and then select the Initial Font button from the Printer Setup dialog box. Choose a font, and select OK. Then select OK and Close to return to your document.

Avoiding the Ransom Note Look

The downside to WordPerfect for Windows' easy-to-use character attributes and fonts is that they can sometimes be *too* easy to use. Flushed with your newfound knowledge, you start throwing every formatting option in sight at your documents. This can turn even the most profound and well-written documents into a real dog's breakfast. (It's known in the trade as the "ransom note look.") Here are some tips to avoid overdoing your formatting:

☛ Never use more than a couple of fonts in a single document. Anything more looks amateurish, and will only confuse the reader.

☛ If you need to emphasize something, bold or italicize it in the *same* font as the surrounding text. Avoid using underlining for emphasis.

☛ Use larger sizes only for titles and headings.

☛ Avoid bizarre decorative fonts for large sections of text. Most of those suckers are hard on the eyes after a half dozen words or so. Serif fonts are usually very readable, so they're a good choice for long passages. The clean look of sans serif fonts makes them a good choice for headlines and titles.

State Your Case: Converting Uppercase and Lowercase Letters

On most keyboards, the Caps Lock key is just above the Shift key. Inevitably, in the heat of battle, I end up hitting Caps Lock by mistake a few times a day. The result: anything from a few words to a few lines all in uppercase! Fortunately, WordPerfect for Windows lets me off the hook easily with its case-conversion feature. You can change uppercase to lowercase, lowercase to uppercase, and you can even get it to convert only the initial letter in each word to uppercase (to change *alphonse* to *Alphonse*, for example).

To convert case, select the appropriate block, pull down the Edit menu, and then select the Convert Case command. In the cascade menu that appears, select Uppercase, Lowercase, or Initial Capitals (version 6 only).

Adding Silly Symbols

Were you stumped the last time you wanted to write Dag Hammarskjöld because you didn't know how to get one of those ö thingamajigs? I thought so. Well, you'll be happy to know that your documents aren't restricted to just the letters, numbers, and punctuation marks that you can eyeball on your keyboard. In fact, WordPerfect for Windows comes with all kinds of built-in characters that will supply you with not only an ö, but a whole universe of weirdo symbols.

To start, position the insertion point where you want to insert the symbol (at this point, it doesn't matter all that much where you put the insertion point). Now pull down the **Insert** menu and select the Character command, or press **Ctrl+W**. A dialog box called WordPerfect Characters will appear on the screen.

The layout is pretty simple: the Characters area shows you all the symbols available for whatever character set is selected in the Character Set pop-up list. If you select a different character set, a whole new set of symbols is displayed.

5.2 fans need to pull down the Font menu, and select the WP Characters command.

To use a symbol from a character set, move into the Characters area and use the arrow keys to highlight the symbol, or just click on it. You then have two choices:

☞ If you want to pick several symbols, select the Insert button for each one.

☞ To add the symbol and then return to the document, select the Insert and Close button.

The Least You Need to Know

This chapter was the first stop on our journey toward looking good on paper. You learned all about fonts and how to format characters with different typefaces, type styles, and so on. Here's the condensed version of what happened:

☞ Fonts are distinctive character designs. They're characterized by four attributes: typeface, type style, type size, and relative position.

☞ To select a different font, choose Font from the Layout menu (or press **F9**) and pick out what you need from the Font dialog box.

☞ If you need to convert a block of text from upper- to lowercase (or vice versa), select Convert Case from the Edit menu, and choose the appropriate command.

☞ WordPerfect for Windows comes with various character sets built-in. These sets can give you international characters, scientific symbols, and more. Select the Character command from the Insert menu.

Chapter 13
Making Your Lines and Paragraphs Look Good

In This Chapter

- ☛ Setting and deleting tab stops in a paragraph
- ☛ Left-justifying, centering, and right-justifying text
- ☛ Adjusting the line spacing
- ☛ Indenting paragraph text
- ☛ Working with paragraph margins
- ☛ The usual motley collection of trenchant tips and topical tirades

The last chapter showed you how to format characters, so now we'll bump things up a notch, and look at formatting lines and paragraphs. How will this help you look good on paper? Well, all the character formatting in the world won't do you much good if your lines are all scrunched together, and if the various pieces of text aren't lined up like boot-camp recruits. Documents like these look cramped and uninviting, and will often get tossed in the old circular file without a second look. This chapter will help you avoid this sorry fate.

When you're working through this chapter, if things somehow go haywire and your document ends up all askew, you need to do two things. First, start chanting the following mantra in your head: "This is not my fault, this is WordPerfect's fault. This is not my fault. . . ." Second, select **Undo** from the **Edit** menu, or press **Ctrl+Z** (**Alt+Backspace** in 5.2) to reverse the mayhem.

Formatting Lines Versus Paragraphs

The way WordPerfect for Windows formats lines and paragraphs can be hopelessly confusing, even for experienced word processing hacks. So, to soften the blow a little, here are some things to keep in mind when working with this chapter's formatting options:

☞ If you select a format option *without* selecting a block, WordPerfect for Windows formats everything from the current paragraph to the end of the document.

☞ If you select a block (even a single character), WordPerfect for Windows formats only the paragraph that contains the block.

Working with Tab Stops

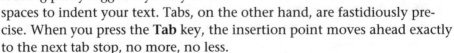

Documents look much better if they're properly indented, and if their various parts line up nicely. The best way to do this is to use tabs instead of spaces whenever you need to create some room in a line. Why? Well, a single space can take up different amounts of room, depending on the font and size of the characters you're using. So your document can end up looking pretty ragged if you try to use spaces to indent your text. Tabs, on the other hand, are fastidiously precise. When you press the **Tab** key, the insertion point moves ahead exactly to the next tab stop, no more, no less.

To begin, pull down the **Layout** menu, select **Line**, and then select **Tab Set**. This displays both the Tab Set dialog box and the Ruler Bar. (That's right, *another* bar; it seems like WordPerfect for Windows has more bars than Hershey's.) The Ruler Bar shows you where the current tabs are set. (The numbers measure the distance in inches from the left edge of the page.) Each of the strangely shaped black marks represents a tab stop.

> ### By the Way . . .
> It's often best to start with a clean slate and just set your own tabs. See the section titled "Deleting Tabs," later on in the chapter.

Checking Out WordPerfect for Windows' Tab Types

As you can see in the screen shown on the next page, WordPerfect for Windows has a tab for your every mood. Here's a quickie summary of the available types:

SPEAK LIKE A GEEK

Tabs preceded by dots are called *dot leaders*.

Left	Text lines up with the tab on the left.
Right	Text lines up with the tab on the right.
Center	Text is centered on the tab.
Decimal	Numbers line up with the tab at their decimal places.
Dots	The tab is preceded by a bunch of dots. These tabs normally line up on the left, but (if you have version 6) you can also make them line up on the right, center, or decimals.

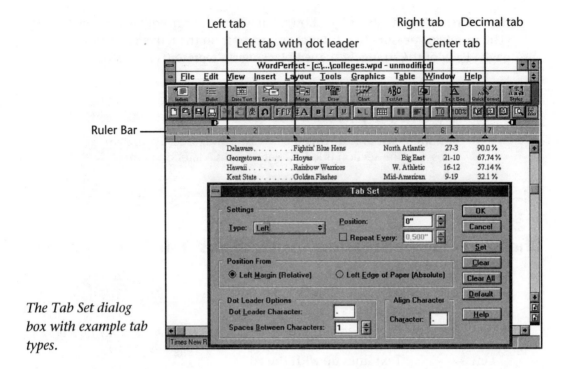

The Tab Set dialog box with example tab types.

Setting Tabs

Once you've displayed the Tab Set dialog box, you can set your tabs by following these steps:

1. Select a tab type from the **T**ype pop-up list.

2. Use the **P**osition spinner to enter a location for the tab. If you want to enter multiple tabs at regular intervals, activate the Repeat Every check box and enter the interval in the spinner beside it.

3. Select the **S**et button. The tab stop appears in the Ruler Bar.

4. Repeat steps 1–3 to set other tab stops.

5. When you're done, select **OK**.

Deleting Tabs

If you'd like to get rid of a tab or two, open the Tab Set dialog box and use any of the following techniques:

- ☞ To delete a single tab, enter its position in the **Position** spinner, and then select the Clear button (or, in version 5.2, Clear Tab).

- ☞ If you want all the tabs deleted to give yourself a fresh start, select the Clear All button (Clear Tabs in 5.2).

- ☞ If you'd like to revert to WordPerfect for Windows' default tabs (i.e., a left tab every half inch), select the Default button.

TECHNO NERD TEACHES

You can also make your tab stops *absolute* or *relative*. Absolute tab stops are measured from the left edge of the page. They're rock solid; they wouldn't change position in a hurricane. Relative tab stops are more laid back. They're measured from the left margin, so if you change the margin position (which I'll show you how to do in the next chapter), they're happy to move right along. In general, it's best to stick with relative tab stops.

Setting Tabs with the Ruler Bar

Setting tabs with the Tab Set dialog box is a bit of a pain because not only do you have to work all kinds of controls, but if you don't like your tabs, you have to open it up and go through the whole process again. (And when you throw in all that rot about "absolute" versus "relative" tabs, well, forget about it.) What the world needs is a simple way to set tabs; one where you could just point and say, "By jove, I want a decimal tab right here!"

Well, it's my pleasure to report that indeed there *is* a simple way to set tabs: the Ruler Bar. Yes, the same Ruler you saw earlier when you ran the Tab Set command. Only this time, once you're freed from the shackles of the Tab Set dialog box, you'll see that this handy tool makes setting tabs as easy as clicking your mouse.

First things first, however. To view the Ruler, pull down the **View** menu and select the **Ruler Bar** command, or press **Alt+Shift+F3**. (In version 5.2, select **Ruler** or press **Alt+Shift+F3**). In version 6, you'll also need the Power Bar, so display it now if it's not already in view (select Power Bar from the View menu).

You can set your tabs by following these steps:

1. Position the mouse pointer over the Tab Set tool in the Power Bar and then press and hold the left mouse button. A list of WordPerfect's tab types appears.

Hold down the left mouse button on this Power Bar tool to see a list of tab types.

Tab Set tool

2. With the left button still held down, move the pointer through the list, select the tab type you want, and then release the button. The picture on the face of the Tab Set tool changes to reflect your selection.

3. Move the mouse pointer into the lower half of the Ruler Bar and then click on the position where you want the tab to appear. WordPerfect for Windows sets the tab.

In version 5.2, you set a tab by dragging one of the tab type buttons (they're on the left, just below the Ruler) onto the Ruler and then releasing the mouse at the appropriate position.

The Power Bar/Ruler Bar combination is good for more than just setting tabs. Check this out:

☞ To move a tab, just drag it along the Ruler Bar with your mouse. As you drag, WordPerfect for Windows thoughtfully displays a dashed line down the screen so you can see how things will line up. It also shows the tab type and your current position in the status bar (see the screen on the next page).

Tab Set tool   Drag the tab markers to move them.

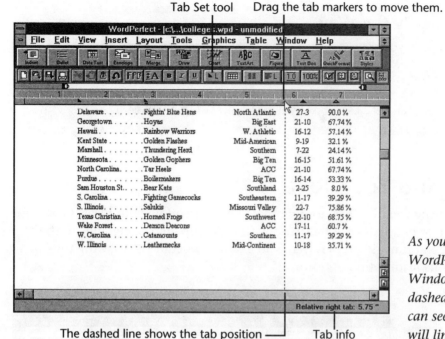

As you drag a tab, WordPerfect for Windows displays a dashed line so you can see where the tab will line up.

The dashed line shows the tab position ——   Tab info

By the Way . . .

To drag a tab, place the mouse pointer over the tab, press and hold down the left mouse button, and then move the mouse to the left or right. (Don't move down, though, or you'll delete the tab!)

☞ To clear a tab, just drag it below the Ruler.

☞ To clear all the tabs, click on the **Tab Set** tool on the Power Bar and select the **Clear All Tabs** option.

> **By the Way . . .**
> If you have version 6, you can right-click anywhere inside the tab area of the Ruler Bar to see a QuickMenu of tab options. You can use this menu to select a tab type, clear all the tabs, or display the Tab Set dialog box. You can also display the Tab Set dialog box by double-clicking on the Ruler Bar.

Justifying Your Text

Justifying your text has nothing to do with defending your ideas (luckily for some of us!). Rather, it has to do with lining up your paragraphs so they look all prim and proper. Here's an example document, showing the various justification options.

Justification tool

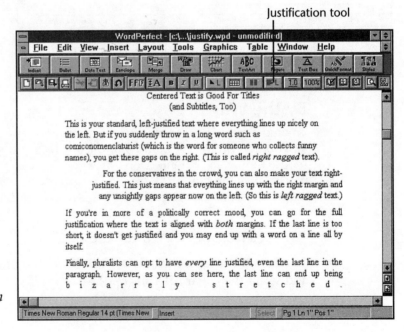

Some text justification examples.

If you pull down the Layout menu and select Justification, you'll see five options for your justification fun:

Left   Justifies each line on the left margin. (You can also press **Ctrl+L**.)

Center   Centers each line between both margins (press **Ctrl+E** in version 6 or **Ctrl+J** in version 5.2).

Right   Justifies each line on the right margin (press **Ctrl+R**).

Full   Justifies each line on both margins. Ignores the last line in a paragraph if it's too small (press **Ctrl+J** in version 6 or **Ctrl+F** in 5.2).

All   Justifies every line in a paragraph on both margins (version 6 only).

If you try to do any of this stuff on a typewriter, you just end up adding to your stomach's ever-growing ulcer population. On a computer, though, it's a walk in the park.

Left-justified text is said to be *right-ragged* because the right side of each line doesn't line up. Similarly, right-justified text is called *left-ragged*.

It's even easier if you use the Power Bar. Position the mouse pointer over the Justification tool, and then press and hold down the left mouse button. Move the mouse down through the list that appears and, when you've highlighted the option you want, release the mouse button. The Power Bar changes to reflect your new selection.

Justification tool

Press and hold down the left mouse button on this Power Bar tool to see a list of Justification options.

Just to make things confusing, WordPerfect for Windows also gives you a way to justify individual lines. To check this out, place the insertion point anywhere in the line and select the Line command from the Layout menu. If you want to center the line, select the Center command from the cascade menu, or press **Shift+F7**. To right justify the line, select the Flush Right command, or press **Alt+F7**.

Changing the Line Spacing

Typewriters have little levers or buttons you can maneuver to alter the line spacing. Well, anything a typewriter can do, WordPerfect for Windows can do better. So, while a typewriter usually only lets you set up double- or triple-spacing, WordPerfect for Windows can handle just about any number of spaces—and even accepts decimals!

To set your line spacing, pull down the Layout menu, select Line, and then select Spacing. In the Line Spacing dialog box, use the Spacing spinner to enter the number of spaces you want. When you're ready, select **OK**.

You can also use the ever-handy Power Bar to set your line spacing. Press and hold down the left mouse button over the Line Spacing tool, and then select a number from the list that appears. If you don't see a number you want, select **Other** to display the Line Spacing dialog box.

Press and hold down the left mouse button on this Power Bar tool to see a list of line spacing options.

 Line Spacing tool

> ## By the Way . . .
> The maximum value you can use for line spacing is 160 (!).

Indenting Text

If you need to indent a whole paragraph from the margin, don't do it with tab stops. Instead, WordPerfect for Windows will indent an entire paragraph for you. Just place the insertion point at the beginning of the paragraph (you don't need to select a block this time—didn't I tell you this was confusing?), select Paragraph from the Layout menu, and then select the Indent command, or press **F7**. WordPerfect for Windows indents each line in the paragraph to the next tab stop.

By the Way . . .

If you want to indent only the first line, see the next section.

If you need to indent a paragraph from *both* margins, place the insertion point at the beginning of the paragraph and select Paragraph from the Layout menu again, but this time choose the Double Indent command, or press **Ctrl+Shift+F7**.

Put It to Work

Indented paragraphs are best used to separate a section of text from the rest of a document. A good example is when you need to quote a long passage. "If you only need to quote a sentence or two, like I'm doing here, just include it in the normal flow of the text." But if it's longer, use a separate, indented paragraph and lead into it with a colon:

> See? By moving the quote out of the regular text, you do two things: you avoid cluttering your prose with a long, rambling quotation such as this, and you also give the quote more prominence (whether it deserves it or not). Notice, too, that you don't need quotation marks. It's understood from the context that this is someone talking.

Whether you indent just from the left or on both sides is a matter of personal choice. Personally, I like using both sides, because it creates a greater sense of separation from the rest of the text. End of style lesson.

Setting Paragraph Margins

Every page in a document has a margin around each side. I'll show you how to work with these in the next chapter, but as a warm-up, let's see how you format a paragraph's margins. A *paragraph's* margins? Yup. This just refers to the white space above and below a paragraph (i.e., the spacing between paragraphs) and to the left and right of a paragraph (i.e., between the paragraph and the left and right page margins). As an added bonus, you can also indent the first line of a paragraph.

Here's how it's done:

1. Select a block in the paragraph you want to work with.

2. Pull down the Layout menu, select Paragraph, and then select Format from the cascade menu. You'll see the Paragraph Format dialog box, shown below.

Left paragraph margin marker   Right paragraph margin marker

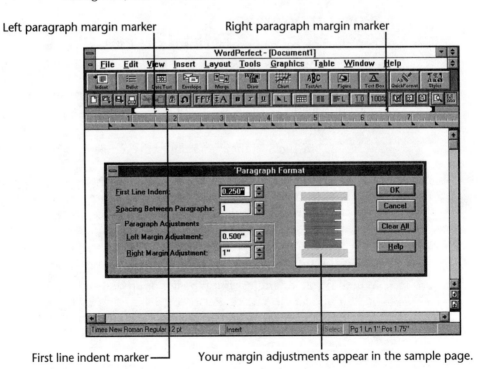

First line indent marker ——   Your margin adjustments appear in the sample page.

3. Use the spinners to select your paragraph formatting options. You should note three things here:

    ☞ First Line Indent adjusts the first line of the paragraph relative to the left paragraph margin.

    ☞ Spacing Between Paragraphs adjusts the number of spaces below the paragraph.

    ☞ The **L**eft Margin Adjustment and **R**ight Margin Adjustment are relative to the current page margins. So if you enter **1"** and the page margins are 1 inch, the paragraph will be indented 2 inches.

    ☞ Keep an eye on the sample page to get a sneak preview of how your adjustments will affect the paragraph.

4. When you're done, select **OK** to return to the document.

Adjusting Paragraph Format with the Ruler Bar

If you prefer a more visual approach to paragraph formatting, the Ruler Bar in version 6 lets you adjust both the left and right paragraph margins as well as the first line indent, with a simple drag on the old mouse.

To see how, display the Ruler (by selecting **R**uler Bar from the **V**iew menu, or by pressing **Alt+Shift+F3**) and look inside the open area just above the Ruler's numbers. Inside, you'll see two small triangles on the left and one slightly larger triangle on the right. (Yes, they *are* hard to see at first. To help out, the screen above shows each triangle moved out from the edges.) They're called *paragraph markers* and here's how you use them to format your paragraphs:

☞ To adjust the left paragraph margin, drag the bottom triangle of the two on the left. Both paragraph markers will move; this is normal.

☞ To adjust the right paragraph margin, drag the right triangle.

☞ To adjust the first line indent, drag the top triangle on the left.

By the Way . . .

Once you have the Ruler Bar on screen, you can also use it to display the Paragraph Format dialog box quickly. Just right-click on the Ruler and select the Paragraph Format option from the QuickMenu.

The Least You Need to Know

This chapter walked you through some of WordPerfect for Windows' line and paragraph formatting options. They are, as I said, somewhat confusing at times, so I think a brief recap is in order:

☞ If you want to format a paragraph, block off some text in the paragraph (a letter or two will do). Otherwise, WordPerfect for Windows formats everything from the insertion point position on down.

☞ To set tab stops, pull down the Layout menu, select Line, and then select Tab Set. Use the Tab Set dialog box to enter your tabs.

☞ To justify text, pull down the Layout menu, select the Justification command, and then choose the justification option you need from the cascade menu that appears.

☞ To change the spacing between the lines in a paragraph, select the Layout menu's Line command, and then select Spacing. In the Line Spacing dialog box, enter the number of spaces you want in the Spacing spinner.

☞ You can indent text either from the left margin or from both margins. Just select the Paragraph command from the Layout menu, and select the appropriate option from the cascade menu.

☞ To set paragraph margins, pull down the Layout menu, select Paragraph, and then select Format. Enter your new margin values in the Paragraph Format dialog box.

Chapter 14
Making Your Pages Look Good

In This Chapter

- ☛ Making adjustments to the page margins
- ☛ Creating your own page breaks
- ☛ Using WordPerfect for Windows' new page mode
- ☛ Adding and formatting page numbers
- ☛ Defining headers and footers
- ☛ Sad stories of widows and orphans

Well, let's see: we've looked at formatting characters, lines, and paragraphs. So, since logic is an occasionally useful tool that I succumb to from time to time, we'll now graduate to full-fledged *page formatting*. This is the stuff—we're talking things like margin adjustments, page numbers, headers, and footers—that can add that certain *je ne sais quois* to your documents. (Of course, adding fancy foreign terms in italics also helps, but I'll leave that up to you.) This chapter takes on these topics and more.

As usual, if any of this formatting stuff gets out of hand, immediately select the **Edit** menu's **U**ndo command to bring everything back in line.

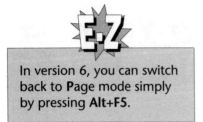

In version 6, you can switch back to **P**age mode simply by pressing **Alt+F5**.

A Note About WordPerfect for Windows' View Modes

This is as good a place as any to talk about WordPerfect for Windows' *view modes*. The view modes determine how your pages look on the screen. Here's a summary (you can select each option from the View menu):

☞ **Page mode**   This is the default view. It shows you exactly what your page will look like when you print it. This includes the document's margins, headers, footers, page numbers, footnotes, and endnotes. You name it, Page mode shows it.

☞ **Draft mode**   This mode hides the top and bottom margins, as well as page formatting, such as headers, footers, and page numbers. You don't see your exact page, but it makes scrolling through the document a lot faster.

☞ **Two Page**   This mode (it's only available in version 6) shows you the big picture by displaying two full pages on the screen at once. You can still work with the pages normally (although you may need a magnifying glass to see what you're doing).

Keep these modes in mind as you work through this chapter, especially when we talk about stuff like headers and footers.

Adjusting Page Margins

The *page margins* refer to the white space that surrounds your text on a page. There are, then, four margins altogether: at the top and bottom of the page, and on the left and right sides of a page. By default, WordPerfect for Windows decrees each of these margins to be one inch, but you can override that, if you like. Why would you want to do such a thing? Here are a few good reasons:

- ☞ If someone else is going to be making notes on the page, it helps to include bigger left and right margins (to give them more room for scribbling).

- ☞ Smaller margins all around mean that you get more text on a page. On a really long document, this could save you a few pages when you print it out.

- ☞ If you have a document that's just slightly longer than a page (say by only a couple of lines), you could decrease the top and bottom margins just enough to fit the wayward lines onto a single page.

Before changing the margins, you need to decide how much of the document you want affected. WordPerfect for Windows adjusts the margins either from the current paragraph to the end of the page, or only for any paragraphs that are part of a highlighted block. So, for example, if you want to adjust the margins for the entire document, place the insertion point at the top of the first page (by pressing **Ctrl+Home**).

By the Way . . .
If you just want to change the margins for a single paragraph, refer to Chapter 13, "Making Your Lines and Paragraphs Look Good," for the appropriate steps.

When you're ready, pull down the Layout menu and select the **Margins** command, or press **Ctrl+F8**. The Margins dialog box appears, as shown below.

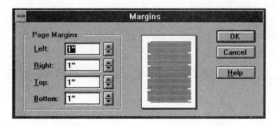

Use the Margins dialog box to set your page margins.

If you plan to print a document on a laser printer, keep in mind that most lasers can't print anything that's closer than a half inch or so to the edge of the page.

You use the four spinners (sounds like a singing group, doesn't it?) to set your margins. For example, to adjust the left margin, enter a number in the Left control. (Note that these numbers are measured in inches from the edge of the page. You don't have to bother with the inch sign (") though; WordPerfect for Windows adds it for you automatically.) If you have version 6, the Margins dialog box also displays a sample page that shows you what havoc your new settings will wreak on your unsuspecting pages. When you're good and ready, select **OK**.

By the Way . . .

When you adjust your margins, you'll notice that the status line's Ln and Pos indicators are affected as well. For example, if you set the top margin to two inches, the **Ln** indicator will display **2"** when you're at the top of a page.

Setting the Left and Right Margins with the Ruler Bar

Our old friend the Ruler Bar makes it easy to adjust the left and right margins. First, display the Ruler by selecting **R**uler Bar from the View menu, or by pressing **Alt+Shift+F3** (in version 5.2 press **Alt+Shift+F3**). Look at the thin strip just above the Ruler's numbers and you'll see two black shapes that look like rectangles someone has taken a bite out of. These are called the *margin markers* and they work like this:

In version 5.2, the margin markers are simple triangles.

☞ To adjust the left page margin, drag the left margin marker.

☞ To adjust the right page margin, drag the right page marker.

> **By the Way . . .**
>
> Once you have the Ruler displayed, you can also use it to crank up the Margins dialog box (provided you're using version 6). You can either right-click on the **Ruler** and select **Margins** from the QuickMenu, or double-click in the margin marker area.

Dealing with WordPerfect for Windows' Page Breaks

As you may know by now, WordPerfect for Windows signals the start of a new page by running a line across the screen (it's called a *page break*). Text that appears above the line prints on one page, and text below the line prints on the next page. This text arrangement is not set in stone, of course. If you insert a new paragraph or change the margins, the text on both sides of the page break line moves accordingly.

But what if you have a line or paragraph that *has to* appear at the top of a page? You could fiddle around by pressing Enter enough times, but WordPerfect for Windows gives you an easier way. Just position the insertion point where you want the new page to begin, pull down the Insert menu and then select the **Page Break** command (or press **Ctrl+Enter**). (In 5.2, pull down Layout and select **Page**.)

Page breaks that adjust themselves automatically are *soft page breaks*. Page breaks that don't move are *hard page breaks*.

Here's a good example of when it's better to be in Draft mode while you're putting a document together. If you insert a hard page break in Page mode, WordPerfect for Windows actually sticks in a whole page, which makes it both slower and more confusing to scroll through the document. To overcome this, switch to Draft mode. The hard page break will appear as a double line (as opposed to the single line of a soft page break), and you'll be able to just scroll past it normally.

To delete a hard page break, you have two options:

☞ Position the insertion point at the beginning of the line below the break and press **Backspace**.

☞ Position the insertion point at the end of the line above the break and press **Delete**.

Keeping Yourself Together

When the last line of a paragraph appears by itself at the top of a page, it's called, sadly, a *widow*. If you get the first line of a paragraph by itself at the bottom of a page, it's called an *orphan*. (No, I *don't* know who comes up with this stuff.) WordPerfect, mercifully, lets you prevent these pathetic creatures from inhabiting your documents. Just pull down the Layout menu, select **Page**, and then select Keep Text Together. In the Keep Text Together dialog box, activate the check box in the Widow/Orphan group.

While we're here, here's a quick description of the other two (occasionally useful) options in this dialog box:

In version 5.2, you can select all this stuff from the **Layout Page** cascade menu.

☞ If you have a block of text that you don't want broken up by an unruly page break, activate the check box in the Block Protect group. (You need to have selected a block beforehand, of course.)

☞ If you want to keep a certain number of lines together, activate the check box in the Conditional End of Page group and enter the number in the spinner. (You need to position the cursor at the beginning of the first of these lines before doing this, though.)

Adding Page Numbers

WordPerfect for Windows' status bar tells you which page you're on when you ramble through a document on-screen, but what happens when you print it out? To avoid getting lost in large documents, you should add page numbers that'll appear on the hard copies. Once you tell WordPerfect for Windows that you want page numbers, the program tracks everything for you.

Everything happens inside the Page Numbering dialog box, so you need to display that first. Just select the **Page** command from the Layout menu, and then select the **Numbering** option.

Positioning the Page Numbers

The first decision you have to make is where you want your numbers to appear on the page. WordPerfect for Windows, ever eager to please, gives you no less than eight (that's right, *eight*) possibilities. To check them out, select the Position pop-up list.

As you can see, most of the options are straightforward. You can position the numbers on the top or bottom of the page, and in each case you can choose from the left, center, or right side of the page. Two other choices—Alternating Top and Alternating Bottom—may require a bit more explanation. These options mean that WordPerfect for Windows will switch the position of the numbers depending on whether the page is odd or even. For example, the Alternating Top option places the numbers on the top right for odd pages and the top left for even pages (which is, you'll notice, the way this book is formatted).

After you've marveled at the sheer wealth of choices available to you, pick the one you want, and WordPerfect for Windows shows what your choice will look like in the sample pages.

Setting Page Number Options

Select the Options button in the Page Numbering dialog box and you'll get yet another dialog box: Page Numbering Options. Two things are of interest to us here:

☞ Rather than just using a number all by itself, you can add some text to go along with your page numbers. So, for example, you could add the word *Page* or even something like *My Great American Novel*. All you do is type what you want in the Format and Accompanying Text edit box. It's usually best to insert the text before the **[Pg #]** code that's already in there.

☞ You can display your page numbers not only as numbers, but as letters and roman numerals (in either upper- or lowercase). Select the **Page** pop-up list and pick out a format that strikes your fancy.

When you're done, select **OK** to return to the Page Numbering dialog box.

Put It to Work

As a rule, you shouldn't work with documents any larger than a couple of dozen pages or so. Not only might you run out of memory, but humongous documents are a pain to work with. Ideally, you should break monster projects into manageable chunks—a chapter per document is usually okay.

Happily, WordPerfect for Windows includes lots of page numbering options that are great for keeping track of these large projects. For example, you can include chapter numbers in your documents. In the Page Numbering Options dialog box, choose the **Insert** pop-up list and select **Chapter** Number. A new code—**[Chp #]**—appears. Add some text so you know which number is which, like so:

Chapter [Chp #] Page [Pg #]

WordPerfect for Windows won't increment these numbers automatically, so you'll need to add them by hand (see the next section). If your project is a multivolume deal (my, you *are* prolific, aren't you?), you can do the same thing with volume numbers.

Setting the Page Number

Most of the time you'll just start at page 1 and go from there. However, you're free to start the page numbers at whatever number you like. This is great if your document is a continuation of an existing project (such as a new chapter in a book). If the rest of the project has 100 pages, then you'd start this document at page 101.

In the Page Numbering dialog box, select the **Value** button. You'll see the Numbering Value dialog box appear. In the Page Settings group, enter the number you want to use in the New **Page** Number spinner. (You can also use this dialog box to manually adjust your chapter and volume numbers, if you have any.) Select **OK** to return to the Page Numbering dialog box.

Formatting the Page Number Font

For truly fancy page numbering, you can format the font just like any other text. Select the Font button in the Page Numbering dialog box, and then fill in the options you want once the Font dialog appears. When you're done, select **OK** to return.

By the Way . . .

Once you've finished setting up all your page numbering options, select **OK** in the Page Numbering dialog box to return to your document. To see your page numbers in action, make sure you're in Page mode.

Centering Text Between the Top and Bottom

If you've read Chapter 13, "Making Your Lines and Paragraphs Look Good," then you know how to center text between the left and right margins. WordPerfect for Windows also lets you center between the top and bottom margins, which is great for things like title pages, resumés, and short business letters.

From the Layout menu, select **Page** and then Center. In the Center Page(s) dialog box, select the option you want and then select **OK**.

In version 5.2, alas, you can only center the current page. Select **Center Page** from the **Layout Page** cascade menu.

Setting Up Headers and Footers

Take a look at the top of the page you're reading now. Above the line that runs across the top you'll see a page number and some text (on the even pages, you see the part number and part name; on the odd pages, it's the chapter number and chapter name). These are examples of *headers*—sections of text that appear at the top margin of every page.

WordPerfect for Windows lets you include headers in your documents, just like the pros. You can put in the usual stuff—page numbers (as described in the last section), chapter titles, and so on—but you're free to add anything you like: your name, your company's name, your dog's name, whatever. And you can even do *footers*, as well. A footer is the same as a header, only it appears at the bottom of each page (makes sense).

To add a header or footer, follow these steps:

1. When you add a header or footer, WordPerfect for Windows uses it for all the pages from the current page to the end of the document. So the first thing you need to do is position the insertion point somewhere in the first page you want to use.

2. Pull down the Layout menu and select the Header/Footer command. The Headers/Footers dialog box appears.

3. You can define up to two headers or footers (A and B) per page. For example, you could have one header on the left (to show, say, the name of the document) and a second one on the right (showing the page number, for instance). So you now need to select which header or footer to add. For example, to define header A, select Header A.

4. Select the Create button. WordPerfect for Windows, as you can see on the opposite page, creates a new header or footer area and, yes, another bar: the Header/Footer feature bar.

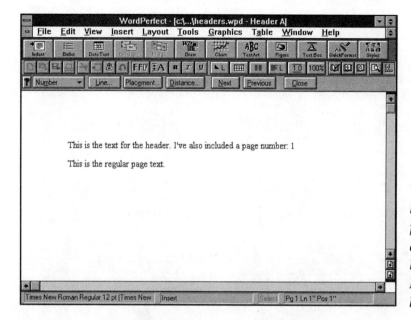

When you create a header, WordPerfect for Windows displays a typing area for the header and the Header/Footer feature bar.

5. Type in the header or footer text you want to use. Feel free to use any character or line formatting options (fonts, bold, justification, etc.). You can also use the feature bar buttons (from the keyboard, you select the feature bar buttons by holding down **Alt** and **Shift** and pressing the button's underlined letter):

Number	Displays a list of page numbering options.
Line	Draws a line between the header or footer and the regular text.
Placement	Displays a dialog box of placement options (odd pages, even pages, etc.).
Distance	Lets you enter the distance to leave between the header or footer and the regular text.

6. When you're done, select Close in the feature bar.

The Least You Need to Know

This chapter walked you through some of WordPerfect for Windows' page formatting options. Here's a recap of what you really need to know to make your life complete:

☞ To see formatting options such as page numbers, headers, and footers, switch to Page mode by selecting the **Page** command from the **View** menu.

☞ To adjust the page margins, pull down the **Layout** menu, select the **Margins** command, and then enter the new margin values in the Margins dialog box.

☞ To add a *hard page break* (one that remains in position even if you enter text above it or change the margins), position the insertion point and press **Ctrl+Enter**.

☞ To add page numbers to a document, first select **Page** from the **Layout** menu and then select **Numbering**. Use the Page Numbering dialog box to set up your page numbers.

☞ If you need to add headers or footers to a document, select the **Header/Footer** command from the **Layout** menu, select which header or footer you want to add, select **Create**, and then add the header or footer.

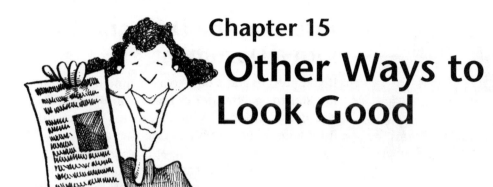

Chapter 15
Other Ways to Look Good

In This Chapter

- ☞ Adding and formatting dates and times in a document
- ☞ Creating footnotes, endnotes, and comments
- ☞ Using hyphenation for fun and profit
- ☞ Working with different paper sizes
- ☞ Miscellaneous ways to fool people into thinking you know what you're doing

This chapter will be your formatting graduate school. The last three chapters covered the grade school of formatting characters, the high school of formatting lines and paragraphs, and the college of formatting pages. Now you get to do post-graduate work with things like dates, footnotes, and hyphenation. Believe me, people will be *very* impressed. Will this be as hard as graduate school? No way. You'll still just be learning the basics in the same non-technical fashion that you've come to know and love.

In version 5.2, the **Date** command is on the **Tools** menu. Select **Text** (or press **Ctrl+F5**), **Code** (or press **Ctrl+Shift+F5**), or **Format**.

Inserting the Date and Time into a Document

If you need to add a date to a document (if you're just starting a letter, for example), don't bother typing it yourself; let WordPerfect for Windows do it for you. All you do is position the insertion point where you want the date to appear, pull down the Insert menu, and select the Date command. A cascade menu appears with three date commands:

- ☞ Date Text   This command inserts the date as though you typed it yourself.

- ☞ Date Code   This command inserts a special code that tells WordPerfect for Windows to always display the *current* date. This means that the date will change if you open the document tomorrow, next week, or next month.

- ☞ Date Format   WordPerfect for Windows has no less than eight date formats, including one that inserts the time only and another that inserts both the date *and* time.

Select Date Text (or press **Ctrl+D**) or Date Code (press **Ctrl+Shift+D**) to insert the date. To get a different date style (or the time), select Date Format, pick out the style you want, and then select **OK**.

Put It to Work

One of the most common uses for the date and time in a document is to keep track of revisions. Some documents may go through a dozen amendments or more, so it becomes crucial to know which version you're dealing with. By including the codes (not just text) for the date and time, WordPerfect for Windows updates everything each time you work on the file, so you always know when it was last modified.

The ideal place for these date and time codes is a header or footer (which I covered in Chapter 14, "Making Your Pages Look Good"). When you're in the header or footer editing screen, just add the date and time as described in this section (make sure you use the Date Code command).

Adding Footnotes and Endnotes

One of the best ways to make people think you worked *really* hard on a document is to include *footnotes* at the bottom of the page. Footnotes say "Hey, this person took the time and effort to write this little parenthetical note for my edification or amusement. I think I'll take her out to lunch."

If you've ever tried adding footnotes to a page with a typewriter, you know what a nightmare it can be trying to coordinate the size of the note with the regular page text. And if you need to change your footnote numbers? Forget about it.

WordPerfect for Windows changes all that by making footnotes as easy as typing text. The program arranges things so your pages accommodate any size footnote perfectly, and it'll even manage the footnote numbers for you—automatically! But wait, there's more! WordPerfect for Windows can also do *endnotes*, if you prefer them over footnotes. Endnotes are less convenient for the reader, but they're good for longer entries that would otherwise take up too much space in a footnote.

Creating Footnotes and Endnotes

Since a footnote or endnote always refers to something in the regular text, your first task is to position the insertion point where you want the little footnote/endnote number to appear. Once you've done that, pull down the Insert menu and select either the Footnote or Endnote command. (In version 5.2, these commands are on the Layout menu.) In the cascade menu that appears, select Create. WordPerfect for Windows displays a special typing area that shows you the footnote number. You also get the Footnote/Endnote feature bar.

Now all you do is enter your text (feel free to use any character or line formatting options). When you're done, select Close from the feature bar. WordPerfect for Windows returns you to the document and displays the same number at the insertion point position.

> ### By the Way . . .
> If you want to see your footnotes or endnotes, put WordPerfect for Windows in Page mode by selecting **P**age mode from the **V**iew menu.

Editing Footnotes and Endnotes

If you need to make changes to a footnote or endnote, select Footnote or Endnote from the Insert menu, and then choose Edit from the cascade menu. In the dialog box that appears, enter the number of the footnote or endnote that you want to edit, and then select **OK**. WordPerfect for Windows displays the appropriate edit screen for you to make your changes. Again, select Close when you're done.

Adding Comments to a Document

When you're writing, you may need to make a quick note to yourself about something related to the text. Or other people may be reading your work on-screen, and they might want to make some snarky remarks for you to see. In either case, you can use WordPerfect for Windows' document comments feature to handle the job. Comments are text that appear in boxes on the screen, but they don't print out.

To add a comment, first position the insertion point where you want the comment to appear. Then select Comment from the Insert menu, and Create from the cascade menu. WordPerfect for Windows displays the comment editing screen (and, of course, another feature bar) in which you can enter your text. You can also format the text and use the following feature bar features:

- Initials   Enters your initials in the comment. (See Chapter 19, "Cool Tools to Make Your Life Easier," to learn how to store your initials and your name permanently in WordPerfect for Windows.)
- Name   Enters your name in the comment.
- Date   Enters the current date.
- Time   Enters the current time.

When you're done, select Close to return to the document. If you're in Page mode, you'll see a small comment icon on the left of the screen. To see the comment, just click on this icon, and WordPerfect for Windows displays the note in a box, as shown below. If you're in Draft mode, the comment always appears in a box.

Comment icon

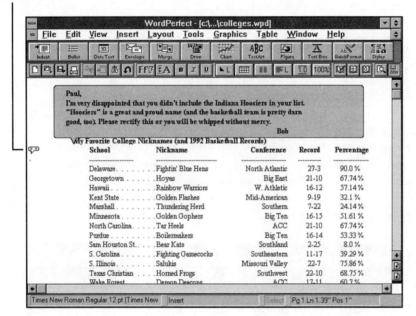

You can add comments to your WordPerfect for Windows documents. These comments don't appear when you print the file.

If you need to edit a comment, either double-click on the comment icon (if you're in Page mode) or double-click on the comment box (in Draft mode).

Put It to Work

One of the keys to productive writing is to build up some momentum. If you're on a roll, but you get stuck on a particular idea or phrase (or if you come across a fact you need to check), don't get bogged down trying to solve it. Ignore it for now and keep going; you can always come back later on and fix things up.

continues

continued

Before moving on, though, you should probably make a quick note or two, just to get your ideas down so you don't forget them. Comments, of course, are perfectly suited to this.

Using Hyphenation to Clean Up Your Documents

As you've seen by now, WordPerfect for Windows' word wrap feature really makes typing easier, because you don't have to worry about a looming right margin the way you do on a typewriter. If you're in the middle of a word when you get to the margin, WordPerfect for Windows just moves the whole word to a new line. While this is convenient, it can make your document look ragged if the word is a large one.

For example, take a look at the first paragraph here.

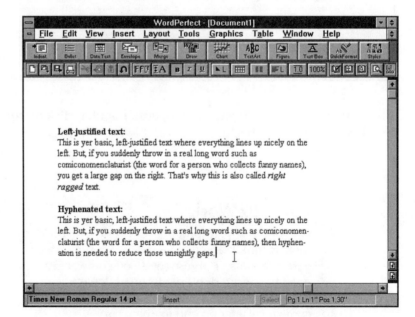

Hyphenation can reduce the gaps produced by some longer words.

As you can see, the second line has a large gap on the right because the next word—*comiconomemclaturist*—was too long to fit. One solution would be to use full justification, in which text is aligned with both the left and right margins. (See Chapter 13, "Making Your Lines and Paragraphs Look Good.") This often works, but you sometimes end up with lines that look unnatural.

Often, a better solution is *hyphenation*, where WordPerfect for Windows takes any long words that won't fit at the end of a line, splits them in two, and adds a hyphen. The second paragraph in our example is hyphenated.

If you just have a word or two you want to hyphenate, forget all this rigmarole. Instead, position the insertion point where you want the word broken, and press **Ctrl+Shift+–** (hyphen). This adds a so-called *soft hyphen*: if you alter the position of the word or margins, the hyphen disappears.

Follow these steps to add hyphenation to your document:

1. WordPerfect for Windows adds hyphenation from the current paragraph down to the end of the document. Position the insertion point appropriately or, if you only want to hyphenate the current paragraph, select a block inside the paragraph (a letter or two will do).

2. Select the Layout menu's Line command, and then select Hyphenation. The Line Hyphenation dialog box appears.

3. Activate the Hyphenation **On** check box and then select **OK**. WordPerfect for Windows examines the text, and if it finds any suitable candidates for hyphenation, it displays the Position Hyphen dialog box that shows you where the hyphen will go.

By the Way . . .

Positioning hyphens in a large document can be a pain. See Chapter 19, "Cool Tools to Make Your Life Easier," to learn how to tell WordPerfect for Windows to hyphenate everything without prompting you.

4. If you don't like where WordPerfect for Windows is going to break the word, click inside the edit box at the location you want, or use the left or right arrow keys to move the hyphen location.

5. Select Insert Hyphen to, well, insert the hyphen.

6. If WordPerfect for Windows finds any more words to hyphenate, you'll have to keep repeating steps 4 and 5.

Working with Different Paper Sizes

You'll probably do most of your work on good old 8 1/2-by-11-inch paper. However, should the mood strike you, WordPerfect for Windows lets you set different paper sizes. For example, you could switch to 8 1/2-by-14-inch legal size, or envelopes, or just about anything you want. You can also select a different *orientation*. Normal orientation has the lines running across the short side of the page, but if you prefer to have the lines run across the long side of the page, you can.

To change the paper size or orientation, select **Page** from the Layout menu, and then select the Paper Size command. You'll see the Paper Size dialog box appear. Select a size from the **Paper Definitions** list. The Information area tells you everything you need to know about the highlighted paper. When you've got the one you want, choose the **Select** button.

SPEAK LIKE A GEEK

Having the lines run across the short side of a page is called *portrait orientation*. When you turn things around and have the lines run across the long side of the page, it's called *land-scape orientation*.

The Least You Need to Know

This chapter took you on a quick graduate course of some other WordPerfect for Windows formatting options. Here's a review before the final exam:

☞ To add either the date or the time to a document, pull down the Insert menu and select the Date command. In the cascade menu, select Date Text to insert a date that won't change, or Date Code to tell WordPerfect for Windows to always show the current date.

☞ Footnotes and endnotes are handy ways to add information to a document without cluttering the text. Select either Footnote or Endnote from the Insert menu, select Create, and then fill in the note. Select Close when you're done.

☞ Comments are an easy way to include notes to yourself or others in a document. Select Comment from the Insert menu, and then select Create from the cascade menu. When the editing screen appears, add your text and then select Close to exit.

☞ Use hyphenation to clean up some of the gaps caused by long words. Select the Layout menu's Line command and then select the Hyphenation command.

☞ To work with a different paper size, select the Page command from the Layout menu, and then select Paper Size. Pick out the paper you want to use from the dialog box that appears.

This page unintentionally left blank.

Part IV
Working with Documents

In WordPerfect for Windows, you don't work with anything so humdrum as a file. Uh-uh. Instead, you work with documents, which—you've got to admit—sure sounds impressive, doesn't it? Why, it's enough to turn even the humblest memo into a virtual magnum opus.

The topics in this part look at the forest of your documents as a whole, rather than the trees of the individual characters, words, and pages. You'll learn about printing (Chapter 16), working with multiple documents and document windows (Chapter 17), and managing files—i.e., copying them, deleting them, renaming them, and more—(Chapter 18).

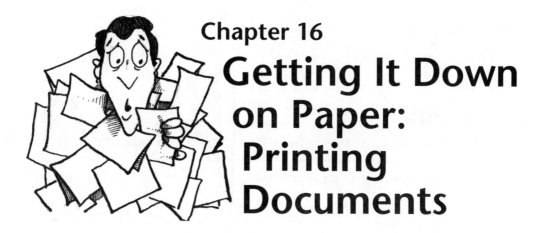

Chapter 16

Getting It Down on Paper: Printing Documents

In This Chapter

- ☛ The basic printing steps
- ☛ Printing a selection of pages
- ☛ Printing an unopened document right from your hard disk
- ☛ Using WordPerfect for Windows' cool Print Preview feature
- ☛ Selecting a different printer
- ☛ Magic, mirrors, movie trailers, and other miscellaneous mumbo-jumbo

Okay, you've managed to peck out a few words on the keyboard, and maybe even gotten used to the idea of not pressing Enter at the end of each line. You've struggled through all those pull-down menus and dialog boxes, you've got a few editing skills down pat, and you've even managed to add a bit of formatting to perk things up a bit. Now what? Ah, now it's hard copy time. Now you print out your creation for all to see. This is one of my favorite parts because, no matter how much I work with computers, I still feel like it's all hocus-pocus—just a bunch of smoke and mirrors. I don't feel right until I see those pages come slithering out of my printer.

To that end, this chapter takes you painlessly through the basics of printing with WordPerfect for Windows.

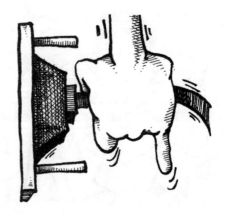

Basic Printing

Without further ado, let's get right to the basic steps that let you print a document in WordPerfect for Windows.

1. Make sure your printer is ready to go:

   ☞ Is it plugged into both the wall and your computer?

   ☞ Is it turned on?

   ☞ Is it *on line*? (Most printers have an "On Line" light that'll tell you. If the light isn't on, press the **On Line** button.)

   ☞ Is there enough paper for your document?

2. Once your printer is warm and happy, you need to decide how much of the document you want to print:

   ☞ If you want to print the whole thing, go ahead and skip to step 3.

   ☞ If you want to print only a single page, place the insertion point anywhere on that page.

   ☞ If you want to print a block, select the block. (You select a block by dragging your mouse over the appropriate text or by holding down **Shift** and then using the arrow keys to highlight what you need. See Chapter 10, "Block Partying: Working with Text Blocks," for details.)

By the Way . . .

WordPerfect for Windows kindly lets you print documents that aren't even open. The section titled "Printing an Un-opened Document" gives you the scoop.

3. Pull down the File menu and select the Print command, or press **F5**. You'll see the Print dialog box, shown here.

Print tool

You can click on this tool in the Power Bar to display the Print dialog box.

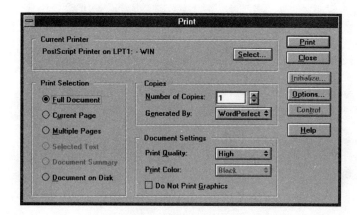

WordPerfect for Windows' Print dialog box contains all the options you need to print your documents.

4. Use the Print Selection group's option buttons to tell WordPerfect for Windows what to print:

    Full Document   Prints the entire document.

    Current Page   Prints only the current page.

    Multiple Pages   Prints a range of pages. See the "Printing Multiple Pages" section later on.

    Selected Text   Prints only the currently selected block.

    Document Summary   Prints the document's summary info, if it has any. (See Chapter 19, "Cool Tools to Make Your Life Easier," to get the scoop on document summaries.)

    Document on Disk   Prints a document right from the disk without having to open it. The section "Printing an Unopened Document" shows you how to do this.

5. If you need more than one copy, enter the number you want in the **Number of Copies** edit box.

6. Use the Print Quality pop-up list to set how nice you want your text to look. If you're printing a final draft, select **High** for the best looking output. If you're just printing out a copy to see how things look, you can save some ink (or toner, if you have a laser printer) by selecting **Medium** or even **Draft** quality.

By the Way . . .

If you want your pages printed in reverse order (which is handy if your printer spits out the pages face up), select the **O**ptions button and, in the Print Output Options dialog box that appears, activate the Print in **R**everse Order check box. You can also use the dialog box to tell WordPerfect for Windows to print only odd– or even–numbered pages. In the Print **O**dd/Even Pages pop-up list, select either **O**dd or **E**ven. When you're done, select **OK** to return to the Print dialog box. (In version 5.2, select the Multiple Pages option from the Print dialog box, select **P**rint, and then select **O**dd or **E**ven from the **O**dd/Even Pages pop-up list.)

If you're printing more than one copy of a multi-page document, consider the **G**enerated By pop-up. This specifies whether WordPerfect for Windows or the printer generates the copies. Suppose you want three copies of a two-page document. If WordPerfect generates the copies, they get *collated*, which means the entire document prints one copy at a time. If the printer does it, the job will print faster, but you'll get three copies of page 1 and then three copies of page 2.

7. When you've finished picking your options, select the **P**rint button to set everything in motion.

Printing Multiple Pages

If you only need to print a few pages from a document, select **Print** from the **File** menu (or press **F5**) and then select the Multiple Pages option in the Print dialog box. When you select the Print button, the Multiple Pages dialog box appears. Use the Page(s) edit box (it's called Range in version 5.2) to specify the pages you want printed. The following table shows you how to enter the page numbers (the letters represent page numbers you can enter):

Use	To Print
a	Page *a*
a, b, c	Pages *a*, *b*, and *c*
a–b	Pages *a* through *b*
a–	From page *a* to the end of the document
–a	From the beginning of the document through page *a*
a, b, f–h	Pages *a* and *b*, and pages *f* through *h*

What's Wrong with This Picture?

To get you more comfortable with this multiple-page printing thing, here are some sample page ranges. Just write in what pages you think will print (assume it's a five-page document).

Make sure you type the page numbers in ascending numerical order. WordPerfect for Windows will choke if you enter something like 8–3 or 6,1.

Page Ranges:

1. 1–2,4–
    Pages printed:

2. 2–4
    Pages printed:

3. 1–
    Pages printed:

4. 3–2
    Pages printed:

5. –4
    Pages printed:

6. 1,2,3–5
    Pages printed:

Answers:

1. Pages 1, 2, 4, and 5 print.

2. Pages 2, 3, and 4 print.

3. Everything prints (pages 1, 2, 3, 4, and 5).

4. Nothing prints (the range has to be specified in numerical order).

5. Pages 1, 2, 3, and 4 print.

6. Everything prints.

Printing an Unopened Document

One of WordPerfect for Windows' nice time-saving features is the ability to print an unopened document. This saves you from having to go through the whole hassle of opening the file, printing it, and then closing it again.

In the Print dialog box, select the Document on Disk option. When you select Print, you'll see the Document on Disk dialog box appear, as shown below. Just enter the name of the file you want to print in the Filename edit box. (If you're not sure of the name, select the list button beside the Filename box and then use the Select File dialog box to pick out the file you want. Select **OK** to return to the Document on Disk dialog.) Enter the pages you want to print, if necessary, and then select the Print button.

Click here to
select the file
from a list.

*Use the Document on
Disk dialog box to
print a document
without opening it.*

Printing Multiple Documents

If you need to print a bunch of documents, you don't have to run a separate Print command for each one. Instead, follow these steps:

1. Pull down the File menu and select Open, or press **Ctrl+O** (**F4** in version 5.2).

2. Select the appropriate drive and directory, if necessary. (See Chapter 7, "Day-to-Day Drudgery I: Saving, Opening, and Closing," to learn how to do this.)

3. In the Filename list, select the files you want to print by any of the following methods:

   ☞ If the files you need are listed consecutively, click on the first file, hold down **Shift**, and then click on the last file.

   ☞ To select files randomly, hold down the **Ctrl** key and click on each file.

   ☞ With your keyboard, highlight the first file, press **Shift+F8**, and then for the other files you want, high light each one and press the **Spacebar**. When you're done, press **Shift+F8** again.

4. In the File Options pop-up list, select Print. WordPerfect for Windows, ever skeptical, asks if you want to print the selected files. Select Print to crank out your files.

Selecting a Different Printer

If you're lucky enough to have more than one printer, you can switch between them in WordPerfect for Windows fairly easily.

You may have noticed when printing that the Print dialog box shows you the name of the currently selected printer in the Current Printer area. To change this, choose the Select button beside it. This displays the Select Printer dialog box, shown on the next page. In the Printers list, use the up and down arrow keys to highlight the printer you want (or just click on it with your mouse) and then choose the Select command.

TECHNO NERD TEACHES

The Printers list will often show two versions of each printer: one with a WordPerfect for Windows logo beside it and one with a Windows logo. What's the diff? Well, these correspond to different *printer drivers* (a *driver* is a small software program that translates WordPerfect's document lingo into codes the printer can digest). Windows has standard drivers for most printer models, but WordPerfect for Windows created their own (probably to make some busy work for an idle programmer or two). The Windows drivers are tried and true, so I'd recommend sticking with them.

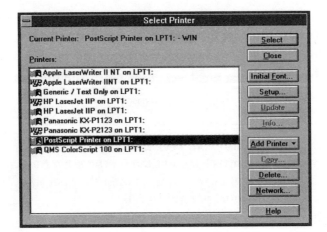

Use the Select Printer dialog box to select a different printer.

The Least You Need to Know

This chapter showed you how to get hard copies of your WordPerfect for Windows documents. Since you'll likely be doing a lot of printing with WordPerfect for Windows, a quick review of the basics wouldn't hurt:

☞ Before printing, make sure your printer is ready for action. Check to see if it's plugged in, the cables are secure, it's turned on (and on line), and that it has enough paper to handle the job.

☞ To print, pull down the File menu and select the Print command (or just press **F5**). Enter your options in the Print dialog box, and then select the Print button.

☞ You don't need to print the entire document each time. If you like, you can print just a block, the current page, or a range of pages. For the latter, select the Multiple Pages option and enter pages you want to print in the dialog box.

☞ To print an unopened document, select the Document on Disk option from the Print dialog box. When you go to print, WordPerfect for Windows displays a dialog box in which you can enter the name of the file you want printed.

☞ To print multiple documents, select **O**pen from the **F**ile menu (or press **Ctrl+O**), select the files you want to print, and then select **P**rint from the **F**ile **O**ptions pop-up list.

☞ To select a different printer, choose the **S**elect button in the Print dialog box, highlight the printer you want, and then choose the **S**elect option.

This page unintentionally left blank.

Chapter 17
Working with Multiple Documents

In This Chapter

☛ The fastest ways to switch between open documents

☛ All about windows

☛ Moving, sizing, closing, and arranging windows

☛ Fascinating juggling lore

Remember the minor juggling craze that bounced around the country a few years ago? Well, your faithful scribe was one of many who jumped on that strange bandwagon. No, I didn't become any kind of expert (or run off and join the circus), but I did learn the basic three-ball pattern. I've kept it up to this day—and will, on a dare, attempt to juggle three of just about anything (which, believe me, has scared the heck out of many a party hostess).

If you missed that particular craze, WordPerfect for Windows lets you do some juggling of your own because you can open as many as *nine* documents at once. This not only lets you work with several documents at once, but it's great for quickly comparing two or more documents, or pasting info between files. Best of all, everything's blindingly simple, as you'll soon see.

By the Way . . .

Nine is a lot of documents, but it's still short of the official world's record for juggling, which is a mind-boggling *eleven* rings at once.

Switching Among Multiple Documents

Opening several documents is easy. Select the File menu's Open command and then select the files you need from the Filename list. Here's a recap of the techniques you can use to make multiple selections in a list:

☞ If the files you need are listed consecutively, click on the first file, hold down **Shift**, and then click on the last file.

☞ For random files, hold down the **Ctrl** key and click on each file.

☞ If you prefer the keyboard, highlight the first file, press **Shift+F8**, and then for the other files you need, highlight each one and press the **Spacebar**. When you're done, press **Shift+F8** again.

Once you have your files opened, you need some way of switching among them. WordPerfect for Windows gives you three methods:

☞ If you can see any part of the document's window, click on it. (I'll explain what a "document window" is later on in this chapter.)

☞ Pull down the Window menu and select the document from the list that appears at the bottom of the menu.

☞ Hold down **Ctrl** and tap **F6** to cycle through the documents in the order you opened them. To cycle through the documents backward, hold down **Ctrl** and **Shift** and tap **F6**.

Multi-Document Possibilities

One of the benefits of multiple open documents is that you can share text among them. There are endless uses for this capability, but here's a sampler:

☞ You could take sections of a report and use them in a memo or letter.

☞ If you have one or more files organized as a project, you could take chunks out and use them to create a summary document.

☞ You could create a document to hold boilerplate (bits of often used text), and keep it open all the time. You could then copy stuff from the file (or add more things to it) at will.

The good news is that this is all extremely simple to do. Here are the basic steps:

1. Open the appropriate files, and display the document that has whatever text you need.

2. Block the text. (If you need some blocking basics, refer to Chapter 10, "Block Partying: Working with Text Blocks.")

3. Use the appropriate Edit menu command to cut or copy the text (this was also covered in Chapter 10).

4. Switch to the document that you want to receive the text.

5. Position the insertion point where you want the text to appear, and then paste it.

WordPerfect for Windows' Adjustable Windows

The window you're currently working in is called the *active window*.

As I've said, every time you open a document, WordPerfect for Windows sets up and displays the file in a new work area. In WordPerfect for Windows parlance, these work areas are called *windows*. This makes some sense, I suppose. After all, at any one time, the screen can only show you a part of a document, so it's like looking through a window at your text.

You can think of your computer as a room with nine different windows. As you've just seen, you can display a document in any of these windows, and switch among them.

Framing a Window

The problem with windows is that normally you can look through only one at a time on your screen. It would be nice, on occasion, to be able to see maybe a couple of documents at the same time. Sound impossible? Hah! With WordPerfect's *window frames*, it's easier than you think. What does framing do? Well, it puts a border around a window that lets you do all kinds of crazy things:

- ☞ Change the size of the window.
- ☞ Move the window to a different location.
- ☞ Make the window really small so it's out of the way.
- ☞ Make the window really big so you can't see anything else.

To access this voodoo, you can either pull down the document's Control menu (by pressing **Alt+–** (hyphen) or by clicking on the document's Control-menu box, as pointed out in the screen shot below, and then selecting **Restore**) or you can click on the **Restore** button (see below).

The Control-menu box and Restore button for a document.

As you can see below, your window becomes smaller and it suddenly sprouts a border with various funny symbols on it.

A framed window.

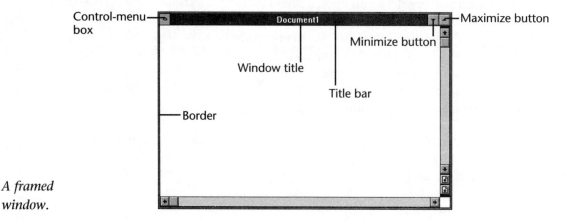

Anatomy of a Window

Here's a summary of the new features you get when you frame a window (I'll talk about things like moving and sizing windows later in the chapter):

Window title. This shows you the name of the document.

Title bar. You can use this area to move the window with a mouse.

Border. This is the window's frame. You use it to change the size of the window with a mouse.

Maximize arrow. You use this arrow to increase the window to its largest extent (i.e., the normal window view you've been using until now).

Minimize arrow. This arrow shrinks the window to an icon.

Control-menu box. You can use the object to move and size a window with your keyboard.

Adjusting Your Windows

Okay, so now you know how to frame a window. I know what you're thinking: How does this affect *me*? Well, it's quite simple, really: a framed window is an *adjustable* window, which means you can move it around, make it different sizes, and more. In other words, you have *control* over what you see on your screen. The next few sections show you how to use that control.

By the Way . . .

Once you start playing around with windows, you'll often end up with a bunch of them scattered willy-nilly about the screen; you may forget which one is the active window. Here are two things to look for:

☞ The blinking insertion point.

☞ The title bar with the darker color.

It's possible to size two borders at the same time. All you have to do is position the mouse pointer on a window corner. When you drag the mouse, the two sides that create the corner will move.

Sizing Up Your Windows

If you'd like to see a couple of windows on-screen at the same time, one way to do it is to change the size of each window so they both fit. This is (by far) easiest with a mouse, but the keyboard will do in a pinch.

The secret to sizing a window with the mouse is to use the *borders* that appear when you frame the window. All you do is drag the appropriate border so it's the size you want. As you're dragging, WordPerfect for Windows displays a dotted line to show you the new size. When things look about right, release the mouse button, and WordPerfect for Windows redraws the window in the new size.

By the Way . . .

Here's a refresher course on dragging the mouse, in case you forgot. First, position the pointer over the object you want to drag (a window border, in this case). Then press and hold down the left mouse button. Move the mouse to wherever you want to go, and then release the button.

If you decide you don't want the window resized after all, just press **Esc**.

If you prefer to use the keyboard, you need to follow these steps:

1. Switch to the window you want to size.

2. Press **Alt+ –** (hyphen) to open the document's Control menu and then select the Size option. A dotted outline appears around the window.

3. Use the arrow keys to size the window outline.

4. Once the outline is the size you want, press **Enter**. WordPerfect for Windows redisplays the window in the new size.

Windows on the Move

One of the problems with having several windows open at once is that they have a nasty habit of overlapping each other. And it never fails that what gets overlapped in a window is precisely the information you want to see. (Chalk up another one for Murphy's Law, I guess.) Instead of cursing WordPerfect for Windows' ancestry, you can try moving your windows around so they don't overlap (or so they overlap less).

Things are, once again, *way* easier with a mouse: all you do is drag the window's title bar. As you do, WordPerfect for Windows displays a dotted outline of the window. When you've got the outline where you want it, just release the mouse button, and WordPerfect for Windows redisplays the window in the new location.

If you use a keyboard, here are the steps to follow:

1. Switch to the window you want to move.

2. Press **Alt+–** (hyphen) to open the document's Control menu and then select the Move option. A dotted outline appears around the window.

3. Use the arrow keys to move the window outline.

4. Once the outline is in the location you want, press **Enter**. WordPerfect for Windows redisplays the window in the new location.

Letting WordPerfect for Windows Do the Work: Cascading and Tiling

All this moving and sizing stuff is fine for people with time to kill. The rest of us just want to get the job done and move on. To that end, WordPerfect for Windows includes Cascade and Tile commands that'll arrange your windows for you automatically.

If you change your mind about moving the window, you can press the **Esc** key at any time to bail out of the move.

By the Way . . .

Speaking of having time to kill, did you know that the world's record for the longest time juggling three objects without a drop is a mind-numbing 8 hours, 57 minutes?

The Cascade command arranges your open windows in a cool, waterfall pattern. This is good for those times when you want things nice and neat, but you don't need to see what's in the other windows. To cascade your windows, select the Cascade command from the Window menu.

By the Way . . .

The basic three-ball pattern that you see most jugglers using is also called a *cascade*. Just a coincidence? I wonder.

The Tile command divides up your screen and gives equal real estate to each window, as shown below.

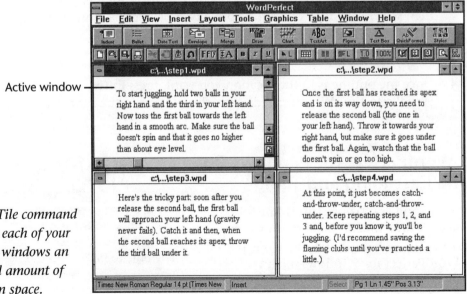

Active window

The Tile command gives each of your open windows an equal amount of screen space.

This pattern lets you work in one window and still keep an eye on what's happening in the other windows (you never know what those pesky little devils might be up to). To tile your windows, select the Tile command from the Window menu.

The Minimalist Approach: How to Minimize a Window

You'll often find you have some windows you know you won't need for a while. You could move them out of the way or make them smaller, but that takes time, and our goal is always to make things as easy as possible. Fortunately, there's an alternative: you can *minimize* the window down to a mere icon of its former self. Here's a picture of a screen with a few minimized windows.

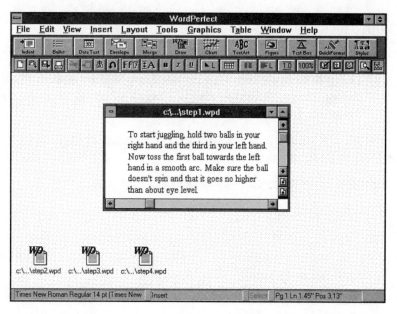

You can minimize a window down to an icon to get it out of the way.

If you use a mouse, you can minimize a window in no time at all, simply by clicking on the frame's **minimize arrow** (the one pointing down).

It takes a bit more effort if you're using the keyboard. In this case, press **Alt+–** (hyphen) and then select the Minimize command from the Control menu.

Taking It to the Max: Maximizing a Window

If you get tired of all this frame monkey business, you can *maximize* a window to its normal size.

If you use a mouse, all you have to do is click on the window's **maximize arrow** (the one pointing up). From the keyboard, press **Alt+–** (hyphen) and then select the Maximize command.

Restoring a Window

When you maximize or minimize a window, Windows is smart enough to remember what the window used to look like. This allows you to easily restore the window to its previous size and position.

With a mouse, you have two options:

☛ If you maximized the window, the Maximize button now appears with double arrows. This is called the Restore button (makes sense, doesn't it?). Simply click on this button to revert the window to its previous state.

☛ If you minimized the window, you restore it by double-clicking on its icon.

From the keyboard, you need to do the following:

☛ For a maximized window, pull down its Control menu, and select the **Restore** command.

☛ For a minimized window, pull down the **Window** menu and select the document from the list.

Closing a Window

You can use the Control menu to close a window quickly with your mouse. All you do is double-click on the Control-menu box. If you've made changes to the document, WordPerfect for Windows will, of course, ask you to save them, as it normally does.

The Least You Need to Know

This chapter gave you the lowdown on using multiple documents in WordPerfect for Windows. You learned some basic techniques for switching among open documents, and for using WordPerfect for Windows' window frames. Here's the highlight film:

- ☞ To switch between documents, either select the one you want from the list at the bottom of the Window menu, or press **Ctrl+F6** to cycle through the documents in the order you opened them.

- ☞ To display a frame around a document window, click on the Restore button or press **Alt+ –** (hyphen) and select Restore from the Control menu.

- ☞ To size a framed window, drag its borders. You can also select Size from the Control menu and then use the arrow keys.

- ☞ To move a framed window, drag the title bar to the location you want. From the keyboard, select the Control menu's Move command and then move it with the arrow keys.

- ☞ If you'd prefer WordPerfect for Windows to arrange your windows for you, select either the Cascade or Tile command from the Window menu.

- ☞ To reduce a window to its smallest size, click on the **Minimize** button or select Minimize from the Control menu. To increase a window to its largest size, click on the **Maximize** button or select the Control menu's Maximize command.

This page unintentionally left blank.

Chapter 18

Managing Files in WordPerfect for Windows

In This Chapter

- ☞ A quick briefing on files and directories
- ☞ Setting up WordPerfect for Windows to work with files
- ☞ Copying, moving, renaming, and deleting files
- ☞ Creating and deleting directories
- ☞ A snappy analogy designed to knock some sense into all this DOS mumbo-jumbo

Most people run Windows programs not only because the fancy-shmancy graphics look good on the screen, but because they don't want to have to deal with DOS. For some, the very *idea* of the DOS prompt is enough to induce big-time fear and loathing.

But the truth is that, sooner or later (hopefully later), you're going to have to deal with DOS in some way. You're going to need to copy or rename a file, or create a directory, or delete the detritus that has accumulated over the years.

But friends, I'm here today to tell you there's good news. I'm here to tell you that, yes, you have to deal with DOS—but, no, you don't have to deal with DOS *directly*. WordPerfect for Windows has built-in features that tame the DOS beast, and while it may not make this stuff any more pleasant, it *does* make it easier. This chapter tells you everything you need to know.

Files and Directories: A Brief Primer

When people ask me to explain files and directories to them (well, no, it doesn't happen all *that* often), I always tell them to think of their computer as a house. Not just any old house, mind you, but one with all kinds of servants waiting to do their bidding. (People usually start warming up to the analogy at this point.) The inside of the house—you can think of this as your computer's hard disk—has maids, valets, cooks, and so on; these are the programs (such as WordPerfect for Windows) installed on the hard disk. Outside the house there are gardeners, landscapers, and chauffeurs; these are the devices attached to the computer (such as the keyboard, printer, or modem).

In the simplest possible terms, your computer's *files* are equivalent to the various elements inside the house. As I've said, the people (the servants) are the files that run your programs. The inanimate objects in the house—the furniture, appliances, utensils, and so on—are the data files (such as a WordPerfect for Windows document) used by you or your software.

Imagine, for a moment, that this house had no rooms, and that all the stuff inside was just scattered randomly throughout. Clearly, trying to *find* anything in such a place would be, if not impossible, at least frustrating. The problem, of course, is that there's no organization. A normal house has many different rooms, and usually everything in one room is related in one way or another. So, if you were looking for either cooking utensils or food, you'd probably look in the kitchen instead of the bedroom. (I said *probably*.)

Your computer's hard disk also contains a number of "rooms," and these are called *directories*. In a properly organized hard disk, each directory normally contains a number of related files. For example, your WordPerfect for Windows directory contains all the files that WordPerfect for Windows uses (and, possibly, some of your documents). You may also have separate directories for other programs installed on your computer.

Let's extend the analogy a little further. Some rooms in a house have a smaller room attached to them (such as a walk-in closet in a bedroom, or a dining room in a living room). Even storage spaces like pantries and cupboards are "room-like" because they store objects. These are examples of what we could call "subrooms." Directories can also have "subrooms," and these are called—you guessed it—*subdirectories*.

Version 6 vs. Version 5.2: Different Approaches to the Same Problem

Programs evolve from version to version, and usually the changes are incremental: a nip here, a tuck there. Sometimes, however, a program feature changes radically in a new version and the old way of doing things no longer applies. Such is the case with this file finagling stuff. WordPerfect for Windows version 6 introduces an entirely different approach from the one used in 5.2. I'll summarize each approach in the next couple of sections and then try to deal with the differences as we go along.

Version 5.2: The File Manager

Version 5.2's file management solution is called, appropriately enough, File Manager. It's actually a separate program that you can crank up from within WordPerfect for Windows. Its whole purpose in life is to make your file and directory chores as painless as possible.

To start File Manager, pull down the File menu and select the File Manager command. You'll see a new window called WordPerfect File Manager, which will look something like (but not exactly like) the one shown below.

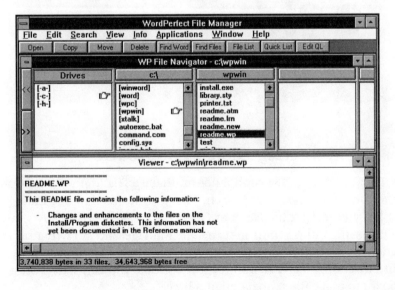

Version 5.2's File Manager.

The File Manager screen looks pretty complicated, but it all boils down to four main features:

Menu bar. File Manager has its own menu bar of file-related commands.

Button bar. It wouldn't be WordPerfect for Windows if it didn't have a Button bar. Like the bars in the regular program, this one gives you quick access to common features with a simple mouse click.

WP File Navigator. These boxes let you maneuver around your disk to find files. The first box (Drives) lists the disk drives you have on your computer. The second box shows the main directory of the currently selected drive (usually C:\). The rest of the boxes show various levels of subdirectories. In each one, you get a list of the contents of the directory (think of it as an inventory of a room on your hard disk).

Viewer. This window shows the contents of the currently selected file.

The basic idea behind File Manager is that you select a file with the WP File Navigator (the Navigator's boxes work just like the lists you've seen in other dialog boxes), and then do something to it (copy it, delete it, whatever).

By the Way . . .

Just to keep us all confused, Windows also has a program named File Manager. It does many of the same things that WordPerfect for Windows' File Manager does, although it lacks some nice touches such as the Viewer window.

Version 6: The "Directory Dialog" Approach

WordPerfect for Windows version 6 doesn't have a File Manager. Instead, it uses the "directory dialog" approach. This just means that any dialog box that lets you select a file (such as Open File or Save As) already shows much of the same information that the File Manager did. So why not let people manage their files right from these dialog boxes? It's more convenient, and by adding a few customization options, you can set up these dialog boxes to make file management a breeze.

In the examples that follow, I'll be using the Open File dialog box. This one's a safe choice because the worst that can happen is that you open a file. If you use, say, the Save As dialog, you might accidentally save your current document under a new name or in a new location.

Customizing the Directory Dialog Boxes

If you have version 6, you can make your file drudgery easier by altering the directory dialog boxes with a few simple customization options.

One big decision you get to make for your file listing is whether to show a regular directory list, a QuickList, or both. A QuickList is a collection of file listings narrowed down to only certain types of files. In our computer house analogy, the normal directory list would be like looking at a complete inventory of, say, the kitchen's contents. A QuickList item for the kitchen might include only the appliances or utensils. To check it out, select **Open** from the File menu (or press **Ctrl+O**) and then select the QuickList pop-up. You have three choices at first: Show **Q**uicklist replaces the normal directory list with a QuickList; Show **D**irectories displays only the Directory list; and Show **B**oth displays both. To get the best of both worlds, I recommend selecting Show **B**oth. When you do, the Open File dialog box changes to look like the one shown below.

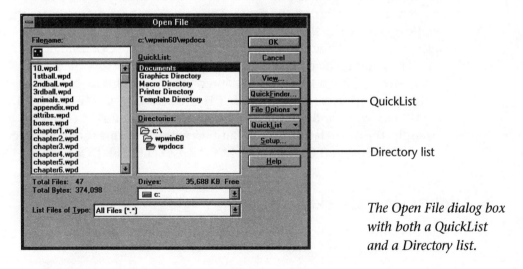

The Open File dialog box with both a QuickList and a Directory list.

As you can see, WordPerfect for Windows displays five predefined QuickList items:

Documents	Displays the files in the WPDOCS subdirectory.
Graphics Directory	Displays the files in the GRAPHICS subdirectory.
Macro Directory	Displays the files in the MACROS subdirectory.
Printer Directory	Displays the files in the WPC20 directory.
Template Directory	Displays the files in the TEMPLATE subdirectory.

To put a QuickList item into effect, highlight it (you'll see its file specification appear in the Filename edit box) and then press **Enter**.

A Word About Wild Cards

To get the most out of QuickLists, you need to know what *wild-card characters* are. In poker, you can designate cards to be "wild" and they can then assume any value during the game. Their electronic counterparts are the wild-card characters that WordPerfect for Windows uses in file names: the question mark (?) and the asterisk (*). The ? substitutes for a single character. For example, the name **chapter?.wpd** would cover any file name where the first seven letters are "chapter," the eighth is anything at all, and the extension is "wpd" (such as CHAPTER1.WPD, CHAPTER2.WPD, CHAPTERS.WPD, and so on). The * substitutes for groups of characters. For example, the name **letter.*** covers all files with the primary name "letter" and any extension (LETTER.WPD, LETTER.TXT, LETTER.DOC, etc.).

Adding Up a QuickList Item

Flushed with this new knowledge, follow these steps to set up your own QuickList items:

1. In the Open File or Save As dialog box, select the QuickList pop-up, and choose **Add Item**. The Add QuickList Item dialog box appears.

2. Use the Directory/Filename edit box to enter the drive, directory, and file specification for the files you want to see in your QuickList item. Here's where you might want to use wild cards. For example, suppose you have a bunch of memos with names like MEMO_15.WPD, MEMO_FW1.WPD, and so on. To display just these files in the QuickList item, you'd enter **memo*.wpd**.

   If you're not sure about what to enter, click on the list button to the right of the edit box and select your files from the new Select Directory dialog box. When you're done, select **OK** to return.

3. Enter a short description of the QuickList item in the **Description** edit box. This description is what will appear in the QuickList list box. In the memos example, you could simply enter **Memos** (see below).

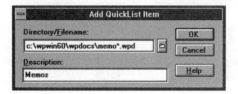

Setting up a QuickList item.

4. When you're done, select **OK**.

> ## By the Way . . .
> If you want to make changes to a QuickList item, highlight it and select the Edit Item option from the QuickList pop-up. This displays the Edit QuickList Item dialog for you to make your changes. To get rid of a QuickList item, highlight it and select Delete from the QuickList pop-up.

> ## Put It to Work
>
> The QuickList is great if you have several people sharing a computer. If everyone uses different files, you can set up a QuickList item for each person so they can easily work with their own files (and keep their grubby hands off yours).
>
> The best way to do this is to create a separate subdirectory for each person (you'll be learning how to create new directories a little later). You can use the person's name to make it clear which directory belongs to whom. When setting up their QuickList item, you use their directory name and the *.* file specification ("*.*" is the wild card way to designate every file in a directory). For example, if one person's directory was C:\WPWIN60\MARGE, you'd enter the following for that QuickList item:
>
> **c:\wpwin60\marge*.***

Customizing the File List

You can also customize the Filename list by selecting the **S**etup button. You'll see the Open/Save As Setup dialog box with the following options:

- ☛ **S**how   This pop-up defines what stuff you see in the file list. You normally see only the file names, but you can also choose to display the file's size and the date and time it was last modified, or you can display "descriptive" names. I'll be showing you how to add descriptive names to your documents in Chapter 19, "Cool Tools to Make Your Life Easier."

- ☛ Sort **B**y   This pop-up determines how WordPerfect for Windows sorts the file list.

- ☛ Sort Order   Select either an Ascending sort (from A to Z) or a Descending sort (from Z to A).

Managing Your Files

Okay, enough messing around. Let's get down to brass tacks and see how you actually do some of this file managing that I've been going on and on about. The following sections take you through some of the more common tasks that'll crop up from time to time. I'm going to assume you're already in either the Open File dialog box (if you have version 6) or the File Manager (if you have version 5.2).

Looking at a Document

I *hate* opening the wrong document. It means that not only have I wasted the time it took to open the file, but now I have to close it and go hunting around for the correct one. What a bother. Happily, you can avoid this fate by actually taking a peek at the file before opening it.

In version 5.2's File Manager, of course, you have the Viewer window to see what your files look like. In version 6, just highlight the file and then select the View button. WordPerfect for Windows opens the Viewer window and displays the file. If you want to view other files, you can leave the Viewer window open and pick out the new file from the Open File dialog box.

By the Way . . .

If you want to see more of a file displayed in the Viewer window, activate the window and then use the usual WordPerfect for Windows navigation keys or, if you have a mouse, the scroll bar. (This is all covered in Chapter 8, "Day-to-Day Drudgery II: Navigating Documents.")

Copying Files

If you need to copy some files to a floppy disk or to another directory, just highlight the files and then do one of the following:

☞ In version 6, select Copy from the File Options pop-up list.

☞ In version 5.2, pull down the File menu and select Copy, or press **Ctrl+C**. (You can also click on the **Copy** button in the Button Bar.)

In either case, you'll see the Copy File dialog box. Enter the destination for the files in the To edit box. (Depending on which version you're using and how many files you selected, this edit box may be called To Directory or Copy Selected Files To.) To be safe, always include the drive and directory. When you're ready, select Copy to start the copy.

Put It to Work

You can use this copying capability as a (very) basic backup command. Place a formatted floppy disk in the appropriate disk drive, highlight the files you want to back up, and then run **Copy**. In the **To** edit box, enter **a:** if the disk is in drive A, or **b:** if it's in drive B.

You can make backing up a little easier by doing the following:

☞ Backing up other files (such as the WordPerfect for Windows program files) will only slow you down. To avoid this, display only documents you've created in the file list (i.e., only those documents with a WPD extension).

☞ Even better, keep all your documents together in a separate subdirectory. Version 6 automatically creates a WPDOCS directory to store your files, so you should use this.

☞ Sort your files in descending Date/Time order. How does this help? Well, the documents you worked on most recently will appear at the top of the list. Since these are the ones you're most likely to back up, it's easy to highlight everything you need and crank up the **Copy** command. I explained how to sort files in version 6 earlier in this chapter. To sort files in version 5.2's File Manager, select **File List** from the **View** menu, then select **Options** from the **View** menu. Use the View Options dialog box to sort your files.

Moving and Renaming Files

If you want to move a file to a new location, or if you want to just give it a different name, highlight the file and do the following:

☞ In version 6, select the File Options pop-up list and then select either Move or Rename. In the dialog box that appears, enter the new destination (if you selected Move) or the new name (if you selected Rename) in the To edit box and then select either the Move or Rename button.

☞ In version 5.2, select Move/Rename from the File Manager's File menu, or press **Ctrl+R** (you can also just click on the **Move** button). This displays the Move/Rename File(s) dialog box and all you do is enter the new name or the new location in the To edit box. When you're done, select Move.

Deleting Files

As you're learning WordPerfect for Windows, you'll probably create all kinds of garbage files while you practice the program's features. This is fine, but after a while these files can really clutter up your hard disk, which makes finding stuff files a real needle-in-a-haystack exercise. You can use the Delete option to do periodic housecleanings. Just highlight a file you want to scrap, and then do one of the following:

☞ In version 6, select Delete from the File Options pop-up. In the Delete File dialog box that appears, select the Delete button.

☞ In version 5.2, select the File menu's Delete, or press **Ctrl+D** (or click on the **Delete** button). This displays the Delete File(s) dialog box, and you just have to select the Delete button to proceed.

Unless you have special undelete software (or at least version 5 of DOS), deleted files are gone for good, so you should be absolutely sure you can live without a file before expunging it. If you have *any* doubts, whatsoever, use the Viewer window to take a gander at the file's contents. (If you have DOS 5 or later and you do happen to delete a file accidentally, you may be able to recover it. To learn how, I'd suggest picking up a copy of *The Complete Idiot's Guide to DOS* by the most excellent Jennifer Flynn.)

Creating Directories

You can add new rooms to your computer house by creating new directories. First select the directory where you want the new subdirectory to appear. For example to add a directory called C:\WPWIN60\MARGE, you'd first select the C:\WPWIN60 directory. Then you do this:

☞ Version 6 users select Create Directory from the File Options list.

☞ 5.2 types select Create Directory from the File Manager's File menu.

In the Create Directory dialog box that appears, use the New Directory edit box to enter the name for the new directory. Then select Create to get things going.

The Least You Need to Know

This chapter gave you a quick tour of WordPerfect for Windows' file management fun. Here's a brief rundown of what was important:

☞ In version 6, you use either the Open File or Save As dialog boxes to manage your files. In version 5.2, select File Manager from the File menu.

☞ In version 6, select Setup to customize the dialog box for easier file management. You can also use the QuickList pop-up to add QuickList items to your directory dialogs.

☞ To work with a file, highlight it and then select a command from the File Options pop-up (if you have version 6) or from File Manager's File menu (if you have version 5.2).

Part V

WordPerfect for Windows Tools

WordPerfect for Windows is one of those programs that you can accessorize. Oh, sure, it looks fine in its basic outfit—but add a bauble here or a trinket there, and you get a whole new look. And the really good news is that this new look also makes WordPerfect easier to use and more powerful. Too good to be true? Nah! Just try on the five chapters in this section for size, and you'll see!

Chapter 19

Cool Tools to Make Your Life Easier

In This Chapter

- ☛ Using the Button Bar to access common commands
- ☛ Customizing WordPerfect for Windows' windows
- ☛ Creating a document summary
- ☛ Customizing the Power Bar, Button Bar, and other such tools
- ☛ Lots of cool stuff that's sure to make users of other word processing programs insanely jealous

I remember a line from a commercial that was on a few years back for some cold remedy: Why suffer through a long cold when you can lessen your misery with *x*?. And so I ask *you*: Why suffer through WordPerfect for Windows when you can lessen your misery with a few tools and setup options? This, after all, has been one of the goals of this book: to help you get your work done with a minimum of fuss and bother. This chapter mines WordPerfect for Windows' menus to uncover a few gems that will allow you to do just that.

The Button Bar: Flexible Command Access

In the bad old days of computers (way back in the 80s!), the only way to run a command in most programs was to press a key or key combination. Users complained because not only was it hard to remember the proper keystrokes, but the hand contortions were crippling people for life.

In response to these complaints, the world's programming geniuses came up with pull-down menus and dialog boxes. These were a big improvement, but then people complained about having to wade through dozens of menus and windows to get the command they need.

So now we have *bars*. Whether they're called "power" bars or "tool" bars or "sushi" bars, they're all designed to give you push-button access to common commands and features. No unsightly key combinations to remember; no menu and dialog box forests to get lost in.

As you've seen throughout this book, WordPerfect for Windows has taken this bar idea to new heights (or lows, depending on what you think of bars in the first place). The Power Bar features WordPerfect for Windows' most common tasks: opening and saving files, cutting and pasting, and so on. The Ruler Bar makes it easy to set tabs and adjust margins. The Feature Bars show up only when you need them (such as when you're creating a header or footer).

Now we're going to look at yet another bar: the Button Bar. Actually, this isn't one bar, but *twelve*! You get the same push-button ease, but each bar is designed with a particular activity in mind. If you're formatting your document's characters, for example, you'd use the Font Button bar (see below). If you're setting up margins and paragraphs, you'd use the Layout Button bar (see below).

The Font Button bar.

The Layout Button bar.

To display the current Button Bar, pull down the View menu and select the **Button Bar** command. To switch among the various Button Bars, right-click on the Button Bar and select the one you want from the QuickMenu. Some Button Bars have two rows of buttons. For these, you'll see a scroll bar on the right side of the bar that you can use to move up and down.

Button Bar tool

You can also click on this tool in the Power Bar to display the current Button Bar.

Who's Zooming Who? Using the Zoom Feature

Normally, WordPerfect for Windows displays your document pages at more or less life size. However, you can enlarge or reduce the size of each page with WordPerfect for Windows' Zoom feature. Just pull down the View menu and select the Zoom command. The following table outlines the various Zoom dialog box options (note that these options have no effect on what your documents look like when you print them out):

Select	To
50% or 75%	Reduce the size of the page.
100%	See the page at normal size.
150% or 200%	Increase the size of the page.
Margin Width	Increase the size of the page so the area between the margins takes up the full width of the screen.
Page Width	Increase the size of the page so the area between the left and right edges (including the margins) takes up the full width of the screen.
Full Page	Reduce the size of the page so you can see the entire page on-screen.
Other	View the page at whatever magnification makes you happy (the maximum is 400% and the minimum is 25%).

When you've chosen the magnification you want, select **OK** to return to the document. If you prefer, you can also select a Zoom option from the Power Bar. Press and hold down the left mouse button over the Zoom tool and then select the percentage you want from the list that appears.

Press and hold down the left mouse button on this tool to display a list of Zoom options.

Zoom tool

Creating a Document Summary

A *document summary* is what you'd expect: a summary of a document's vital statistics: when it was created, who wrote it, the subject matter, and so on. You can also include a descriptive name for the file and then use this name in the Open File or Save As dialog boxes in place of (or in addition to) the cryptic 8-character name required by DOS. (See Chapter 18, "Managing Files in WordPerfect for Windows," for details.)

You display the Document Summary dialog box in version 5.2 by selecting **D**ocument from the **L**ayout menu, and then selecting **S**ummary.

Creating a Document Summary

To create a summary for the current document, pull down the File menu and select the Document Summary command. You'll see the Document Summary dialog box appear (see the next page). This is a fairly simple affair, as dialog boxes go. It's mostly edit boxes and you just fill in the blanks. In version 6, the scroll bar displays more fields, and the icon beside the Creation Date edit box displays a calendar from which you can select the appropriate date. That's about it, really.

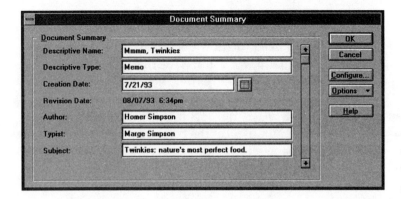

*Use the Document
Summary dialog box
to enter an overview
of your document.*

Customizing the Document Summary Dialog Box

If you have version 6, you can customize the fields in the Document
Summary dialog box. Just select the Configure button and WordPerfect for
Windows displays the Document Summary Configuration dialog box.
Here's how it works:

- ☞ The Selected Fields list shows, in order, the fields currently displayed in the Document Summary dialog box. To change the
order, just use your mouse to drag a field to a different location.

- ☞ The Available Fields list shows all the fields that you can use in
the Document Summary dialog box. Fields that are checked are
currently selected. You can toggle fields on and off simply by
clicking on them.

- ☞ When you've got your new configuration, you can use it as the
default configuration in all your document summaries by activating the Use as Default button.

When you're done, select **OK** to return to the Document Summary
dialog box.

In version 5.2, you can get a word count by selecting the **W**ord Count command from the **T**ools menu.

Getting Document Info

If you need to know document statistics, such as how many words it has, or the average number of words in a sentence (hey, it could happen), select the Document Info command from the File menu. This displays the Document Information dialog box that tallies up the total number of words, lines, and paragraphs and, yes, even calculates the average number of words in each sentence. When you've finished digesting the information, select **OK** to return to the document.

Using Abbreviations

My sources tell me that a place in New Zealand has the record for the longest name: a finger-deadening 85 letters! Imagine having to type *that* all day long. Actually, if they have WordPerfect for Windows version 6, they don't have to. Why? Because the new Abbreviation feature lets you designate a short abbreviation for long or frequently used terms (such as your company name). All you do is type the abbreviation and then tell WordPerfect for Windows to expand it to its full form. This is useful with a capital *U*.

> ## By the Way . . .
>
> For the curious, here's that New Zealand place name in all its glory:
> Taumatawhakatangihangakoauauotamateaturipukakapiki-maungahoro-nukupokaiwhenuakitanatahu. It means, in case you're wondering, "The place where Tamatea, the man with the big knees, who slid, climbed and swallowed mountains, known as landeater, played his flute to his loved one."

As an added bonus, it's also incredibly easy to use. You first select the word or phrase you want to abbreviate. Then select Abbreviations from the Insert menu to display the Abbreviations dialog box. Select Create and then enter a short abbreviation in the Abbreviation Name edit box. Select **OK** to return to Abbreviations, and then choose the Close button.

Once you've defined an abbreviation, just type it, place the insertion point anywhere inside or immediately to the right of the abbreviation, and then press **Ctrl+A**. (You can also select Abbreviations from the Insert menu, select the abbreviation from the Abbreviations list box and then choose the Expand button.)

Getting the Most from WordPerfect for Windows' Bars

As you've seen throughout this book, WordPerfect for Windows has a bar for your every mood. Once you get used to them, you'll find they save you oodles of time and make your life just plain easier. And although most of them work just fine as is, they're all customizable to a greater or lesser extent. The next few sections look at a few of these customization options.

Customizing the Status Bar

The default status bar shows you the current font, whether or not text is selected, and the insertion point position. This is a good start, but there's more info you might want to see (such as the date or time, or whether you're in Typeover mode). You can add new stuff to the status bar, and even change the position of things, by following these steps:

1. Select Preferences from the File menu to display the Preferences dialog box.

2. Select Status Bar from the Preferences menu, or double-click on the **Status Bar** icon. WordPerfect for Windows displays the Status Bar Preferences dialog box, as shown on the following page.

By the Way . . .

You can also display the Status Bar Preferences dialog box by right-clicking on the **status bar** and selecting **Preferences** from the QuickMenu.

Use the Status Bar Preferences dialog box to customize your status bar.

3. The check boxes in the **Status Bar Items** list show you everything you can include in the status bar. Items that are checked are the ones currently displayed in the status bar.

   To add an item, find it in the list and then either click on it, or highlight it and press the **Spacebar.**

   To delete a checked item, click on it again or highlight it and press the **Spacebar.**

4. To change the look of the status bar, choose the **Options** button to display the Status Bar Options dialog box. Make your selection for the font and appearance and then select **OK.**

5. When you're done with the Status Bar Preferences, select **OK** to return to Preferences. Select Close to return to the document.

When the Status Bar Preferences dialog box is displayed, you can also use the following mouse techniques to customize the status bar:

- ☞ To delete an item, drag it off the status bar.
- ☞ To move an item, drag it to the new location.
- ☞ To change the size of the status bar boxes, drag the edges.

Customizing the Power Bar

The Power Bar is chock-full of useful tools, but they may not be the tools *you* use every day. You can remedy this by customizing the Power Bar to suit the way you work. Here's how it's done:

1. Select Preferences from the File menu.

2. In the Preferences dialog box, select Power Bar from the Preferences menu, or double-click on the **Power Bar** icon. The Power Bar Preferences dialog box appears.

> ## By the Way . . .
> You can also right-click on the **Power Bar** and select Preferences from the QuickMenu to display the Power Bar Preferences dialog box.

3. This dialog box is similar to the one you used for the status bar. The available tools are shown as check boxes in the **Items** list.

   To add a tool, find it in the list and then either click on it, or highlight it and press the **Spacebar**.

   To delete a checked item, click on it again or highlight it and press the **Spacebar**.

4. When you're done, select **OK** to return to the document.

You can also use the following mouse techniques to customize the Power Bar when the Power Bar Preferences dialog box is on-screen:

☞ To delete a tool, drag it off the Power Bar.

☞ To move a tool, drag it to the new location.

☞ To insert a space between tools, drag the Spacer icon from the dialog box onto the Power Bar.

Customizing the Button Bar

If you liked the Button Bars we covered earlier in this chapter, you can customize them to make them a little more convenient. First display the Button Bar and then access the Button Bar Preferences dialog box by doing one of the following:

☞ Select Preferences from the File menu and then either select Button Bar from the Preferences menu or double-click on the **Button Bar** icon.

☞ Right-click on the **Button Bar** and select Preferences from the QuickMenu.

> You can also move a Button Bar with your mouse. Just position the pointer over an empty space in the Button Bar. When you see the pointer change to a hand, drag the Button Bar to the location you want.

Now select the Options button to display the Button Bar Options dialog box. You can change the button font and the number of rows displayed on each bar, and you can also do the following:

☞ In the Appearance group, you can control the look of each button by selecting **Text**, **Picture**, or **Picture and Text**.

☞ The Location group lets you specify where the Button Bars appear. You normally see them at the top of the screen, but you can also choose either **Bottom**, **Left**, or **Right**. The **Palette** option gives a free floating Button Bar.

When you're done, select **OK** to return to the Button Bar Preferences dialog and then select Close.

Customizing the WordPerfect for Windows Environment

The bars aren't the only things you can customize. WordPerfect for Windows' *environment* is a miscellaneous collection of items that cover various aspects of the program's operation. To take a look at them, select Preferences from the File menu and then either select Environment from the Preferences menu or double-click on the **Environment** icon. This displays the Environment Preferences dialog box, shown on the opposite page:

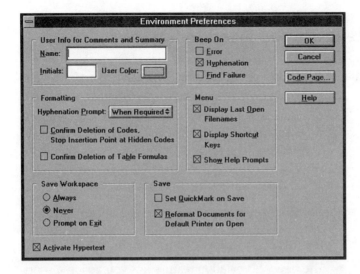

Use the Environment Preferences menu to control various WordPerfect for Windows options.

There are all kinds of little goodies in this dialog box, but here are some of the highlights:

☛ If you use the Comments feature, fill in your Name and Initials. This lets you insert them with the click of a button from the Comments Feature bar (see Chapter 15, "Other Ways to Look Good").

☛ If you like to hyphenate your documents (as described in Chapter 15), but you hate being constantly prompted, select Never from the Hyphenation Prompt pop-up list.

☛ If you find yourself using the same documents day after day, activate the Display Last Open Filenames check box. This gives you a list at the bottom of the File menu of the last four documents you used. You can open any of these documents simply by selecting them from the list.

☛ The QuickMark feature (see Chapter 8) is a handy way to navigate a document. If you like to use it, activate the Set QuickMark on Save check box. This sets a QuickMark at the current insertion point position whenever you save your document.

The Least You Need to Know

This chapter took you through a few neat features designed to make your WordPerfect life easier. Here's a recap:

- ☞ The Button Bar puts all kinds of WordPerfect commands only a mouse-click away. You display it by selecting the **B**utton Bar command from the **V**iew menu.

- ☞ Use the Zoom feature to see your documents from all angles. Select **Z**oom from the **V**iew menu.

- ☞ Document summaries are an easy way to record a document's vital statistics for posterity. Select the **F**ile menu's Document Summary command.

- ☞ The new Abbreviation feature lets you assign a short abbreviation to long words or phrases. Select Abbreviations from the **I**nsert menu.

- ☞ To customize WordPerfect for Windows, select Preferences from the **F**ile menu and choose an option from the Preferences dialog box.

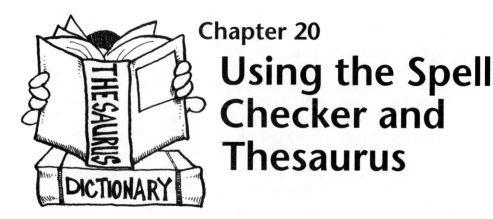

Chapter 20

Using the Spell Checker and Thesaurus

In This Chapter

- ☛ Checking your spelling with Speller
- ☛ Handling unusual capitalizations and duplicate words
- ☛ Using WordPerfect for Windows' Thesaurus
- ☛ A downright fascinating collection of word words

Words. Whether you're a logophile (a lover of words) or a logophobe (one who has an aversion to words), you can't leave home without 'em. Whether you suffer from logomania (the excessive use of words) or logographia (the inability to express ideas in writing), you can't escape 'em. So far, you've seen ways to edit words, ways to organize them, and ways to get them all dressed up for the prom, but when it comes down to using them, well, you're on your own. Now that changes, because in this chapter you'll learn about a couple of tractable tools—Speller and Thesaurus—that'll help you become word-wise (or perhaps even word-perfect). Who knows? With these tools in hand, you may become a full-fledged logolept (a word maniac).

Checking Out WordPerfect for Windows' Speller

Nothing can ruin the image of your finely crafted documents more than a few spelling mistakes. In the old days, we could just shrug our shoulders and mumble something about never being good at spelling. With WordPerfect for Windows, though, you have no excuses because the darn program comes with a utility called Speller—a built-in spell checker. Speller's electronic brain is stuffed with a 100,000-word strong dictionary that it uses to check your spelling attempts. If it finds something that isn't right, it'll let you know, and give you a chance to correct it. You can even add your own words to Speller's dictionary.

You should save your document before running Speller. Not only might you be making a lot of changes to the document, but it takes time—and if a power failure should hit, you'll lose all your changes.

Cranking Up Speller

Speller can check a single word, a block, a page, everything from the insertion point to the end of the document, or the entire document. So the first thing you need to do is position the insertion point appropriately:

☞ If you're checking a word or page, place the insertion point anywhere in the word or page.

☞ If you're checking a block, select the block.

By the Way . . .

You select a block by pressing **Shift** and then using the arrow keys to highlight the text. With a mouse, just drag the pointer over the text. Chapter 10, "Block Partying: Working with Blocks of Text," is where you need to look for more block basics.

☞ If you want Speller to check everything from the insertion point, make sure the insertion point is where you want it to be.

To use Speller, pull down the Tools menu and select the **S**peller command. The Speller dialog box appears. Pull down Speller's Check menu and select how much of the document you want to check. When you feel up to it, select the Start button to get things cranked up.

Speller tool

You can also click on this tool in the Power Bar to start Speller.

By the Way . . .

You can also start Speller by right-clicking inside the typing area and selecting Speller from the QuickMenu.

Correcting Spelling Mistakes

If Speller finds something amiss in your document, it will highlight the word in the text and display the word in the Speller dialog box along with some suggested alternatives, as shown here.

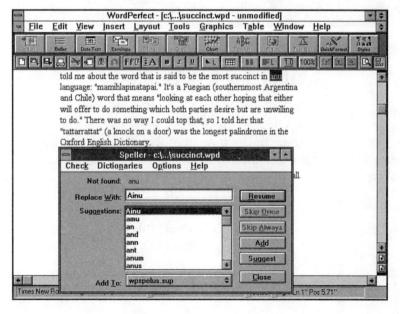

Speller tells you "Word Not Found" when it finds a word that's not in its vocabulary.

If you want to use one of Speller's suggestions, highlight the word in the Suggestions list and then select the **R**eplace button. If you don't see the word you want among Speller's alternatives, you can type your own in the Replace **W**ith edit box and then select **R**eplace.

There are times, however, when a word that Speller doesn't recognize is perfectly legitimate (such as your name, your company's name, or too-hip words such as *cowabunga*). In these cases, Speller gives you three options:

☛ Select Skip **O**nce to skip this instance of the word.

☛ Select Skip **A**lways to skip all instances of the word in the document.

☛ Select **A**dd to include the word in Speller's vocabulary.

By the Way . . .

Speller is good, but it's not *that* good. In particular, it won't flag words that are merely *misused* (as opposed to misspelled). For example, Speller is perfectly happy with either "we're going wrong" or "were going wrong," since everything is spelled correctly. For this grammatical stuff, see Chapter 21, "Painless Grammar Checking."

While Speller is a handy tool, its big problem, of course, is that it won't tell you the meaning of a word. For that you're going to have to rely on a good old-fashioned dictionary. And since Speller isn't infallible, don't treat it as a substitute for a thorough proofreading.

Setting Speller's Options

Speller comes with a few options to check for things beside misspellings. Here's a quick rundown on some of the more useful commands on the Options menu:

Words with Numbers   If your document contains words with numbers in them (such as *Fireball XL-5*), turn off this command to tell Speller not to flag these sorts of words.

Duplicate Words When you activate this option, Speller looks out for the same word twice in in a row (like that). In this case, Speller highlights the second word, and displays a dialog box. Select Replace to fix the problem. If the duplication is okay (for example, Pago Pago or "Tora, Tora, Tora!"), select Skip Once, instead.

Irregular Capitalization If you leave the Shift key down a split second too long, you'll end up with words like "SHift" and "TIerra del FUego." When this command is activatated, Speller will flag these unusual capitalizations and display some suggestions.

Using the Splendiferous Thesaurus

Did you know that the English language boasts about 616,500 words (plus about another 400,000-or-so technical terms)? So why use a boring word like *boring* when gems such as *prosaic* and *insipid* are available? What's that? Vocabulary was never your best subject? No problemo. WordPerfect for Windows' built-in Thesaurus can supply you with enough synonyms (words with the same meaning) and even antonyms (words with the opposite meaning) to keep even the biggest word hound happy.

Starting the Thesaurus

To see what the Thesaurus can do, place the insertion point inside a word, pull down the Tools menu, and then select Thesaurus. WordPerfect for Windows highlights the word and then displays the Thesaurus dialog box, shown on the following page.

Thesaurus tool

Click on this tool in the Power Bar to start the Thesaurus.

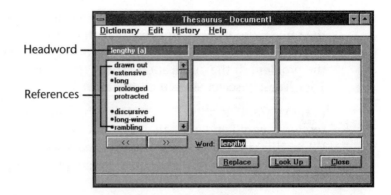

Headword

References

*The Thesaurus
dialog box.*

The word at the top of the column is called the *head-word*. The words in the list are called *references*.

The Thesaurus displays your word at the top of the first column, and displays a list of words beneath it. Depending on the word you used, the list will be divided in up to four different sections: adjectives (a), verbs (v), nouns (n), and antonyms (ant). You can use the **up** or **down arrow** keys or the scroll bar to navigate the list. If you see a word you'd like to use instead of the original, highlight it, and then select the Replace option.

Displaying More Words

If you get lost among the columns, pull down the History menu and select the headword you want to switch to.

Not all of the reference words will have exactly the same meaning as the headword. You can often get more ideas by asking the Thesaurus to display the synonyms for one of the reference words. To do this, just highlight the reference word and press **Enter**, or double-click on it. The Thesaurus displays a new list of words in the next column.

If you like, you can keep repeating this process to get new lists of words in other columns as well. To navigate between the columns of words, use the left and right arrow keys, or click on the left and right arrows in the Thesaurus dialog box.

The Least You Need to Know

This chapter showed you how to get control of your words with WordPerfect for Windows' Speller and Thesaurus utilities. Here's a quick review for the logofascinated:

☞ To start Speller, select **S**peller from the **T**ools menu. Once the Speller dialog box appears, use the options in the Che**c**k menu to select how much of the document you want to check.

☞ To correct a spelling mistake found by Speller, either edit the word in the Replace **W**ith box or highlight one of Speller's suggestions, and then select **R**eplace.

☞ If a word flagged by Speller is actually spelled correctly, you can select the **A**dd button to include the word in Speller's vocabulary.

☞ WordPerfect for Windows' Thesaurus can give you a list of synonyms and antonyms for a word. Just place the insertion point inside the word and select the **T**ools menu's Thesaurus command.

This page unintentionally left blank.

Chapter 21
Painless Grammar Checking

In This Chapter

- About Grammatik, WordPerfect for Windows' grammar checker
- Using Grammatik to check your documents interactively
- Fixing (or ignoring) grammatical errors
- Allowing for different writing styles
- Idiot-proof grammar checking that absolutely *doesn't* require you to know a thing about predicates or prepositions

Grammar ranks right up there with *root canal* and *tax audit* on most people's Top Ten Most Unpleasant Things list. And it's no wonder, too: all those dangling participles, passive voices, and split infinitives. One look at that stuff and the usual reaction is "Yeah, well split *this!*"

If, like me, you couldn't tell a copulative verb from a correlative conjunction if your life depended on it, help is just around the corner. WordPerfect for Windows comes with a tool *that will check your grammar for you.* That's right, this utility—it's called Grammatik—will actually analyze your document phrase by phrase, sentence by sentence, and tell you if things aren't right. It'll even tell you how to fix the problem, and often will be able to do it for you at the press of a key. It's about as painless as grammar gets, and it's the subject of this chapter.

Starting Grammatik

Before starting Grammatik, open or switch to the document you want to check. Grammatik can check a single sentence, a block, a paragraph, everything from the cursor to the end of the document, or the entire document. So the first thing you need to do is position the cursor appropriately:

☞ If you're checking a sentence or paragraph, place the insertion point inside the sentence or paragraph.

☞ If you're checking a block, select the block.

☞ If you want Grammatik to check everything from the insertion point, make sure the insertion point is where you want it to be.

Now pull down the Tools menu and select the Grammatik command. Press **Start** and Grammatik immediately starts checking your document's grammar and, if it finds a problem, it displays the Grammatik window, shown here.

You can also click on this tool in the Power Bar to start Grammatik.

Grammatik tool

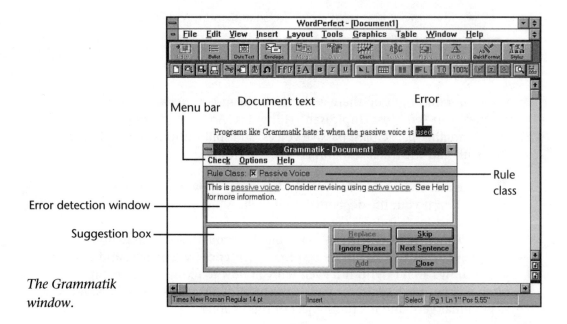

The Grammatik window.

The Grammatik window contains the following sections:

Menu bar   These menus let you control Grammatik's settings.

Rule class   Grammatik divides grammar problems into more than 60 different types or *classes*. This line tells you which class the current problem falls under.

Error detection window   This shows you the grammar faux pas in your document that caused Grammatik to go "tsk, tsk." It also tells you what Grammatik thinks you ought to do about it.

Suggestion box   This is where Grammatik suggests replacements for the errant prose. You'll see this only on certain types of problems.

Once the Grammatik window appears, you may need to use the commands on the Check menu to tell Grammatik how much of the document to check. If you selected a block, Grammatik defaults to the Selected Text option. Otherwise, Grammatik selects Document. If neither of these is what you want, you can also choose Sentence, Paragraph, or To End of Document.

Handling Grammatik's Errors

Once Grammatik displays an error, you need to decide what the heck to do with it. In some cases, the problems Grammatik finds are the result of a typing boner. In this case, you can edit the document text directly and then resume Grammatik.

By the Way . . .

Just because Grammatik says something is a problem, doesn't mean it actually *is* a problem. See the section "A Word About Grammatik's Accuracy," later in the chapter.

In other cases, Grammatik may flag problems in a rule class that you don't care about. For example, Grammatik will usually scold you for using

TECHNO NERD TEACHES

The grammar hounds in the audience (or just those who are gluttons for punishment) might want to check out the **Help** menu's Show Parts of Speech command. This displays the various parts of speech (nouns, verbs, conjunctions, and so on) that Grammatik has assigned to the words in the problem sentence. For an explanation of the weird abbreviations, select **Contents** from the **Help** menu and then select the **Show Parts of Speech** topic.

clichés in your writing. If you happen to *like* using clichés, you can tell Grammatik to shut up about them by deactivating the Rule Class check box the next time a cliché error appears.

The rest of your choices are handled by the buttons in the Grammatik window:

☛ **Replace**   This command tells Grammatik to fix the problem using its suggested replacement. If the problem is a spelling error, you'll see a list of possible words. In this case, highlight the word you want and press **Enter**.

☛ **Skip**   This command (one of my favorites) just ignores the problem altogether and tells Grammatik to move on.

☛ **Ignore Phrase**   This command tells Grammatik not to flag any other instances of the highlighted phrase. In some cases, this button may say **Ignore Word**, instead.

☛ Next Sentence   This tells Grammatik to skip the current sentence and move on to the next one.

☛ Resume   If you pause Grammatik (say, to edit some text in the document), this button cranks Grammatik back up again.

☛ Close   When you've had enough of independent clauses and indefinite pronouns, this button shuts down the Grammatik window and returns you to your document.

By the Way . . .

Some of Grammatik's explanations can get pretty technical. If you feel brave enough, you can look up some of the more arcane terms in Grammatik's glossary. Select **Contents** from the **Help** menu, and then select the **Glossary** option from the Help window. In the list that appears, click on the word or phrase, or highlight it (by pressing **Tab**) and press **Enter**.

A Word About Grammatik's Accuracy

Grammatik is probably one of the most sophisticated software programs on the market today. As you've seen, it can do some pretty amazing things—but in the end, it's no match for the English language. There are just too many strange rules, and too many ways to throw sentences together. As a result, Grammatik will often either miss some obvious problems, or flag things that are okay.

The screen below shows an example where Grammatik missed a glaring error, but flagged something that was fine.

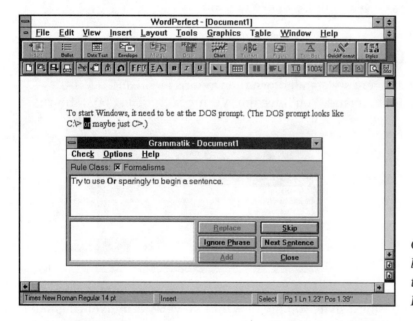

Grammatik is good, but it's no match for the complexity of English.

The phrase "it need to be" is bad English in anyone's books (except, possibly, for the bogus Indians in Grade-B westerns), but Grammatik missed it completely. On the other hand, it thinks that the "or" is starting a new sentence. (It was probably thrown off by the prompt symbol C:\>. It seems DOS messes with *everyone's* head!)

The lesson here is not that Grammatik is a lousy program, because it's not. It's just that you shouldn't lean on it too heavily. Take Grammatik's advice with a grain of salt, and always proofread your work yourself.

Working with Writing Styles

Obviously, not all documents are created equal. Some are stiff and formal, while others are relaxed and jaunty (and others, like portions of this book, are just downright silly). Each of these styles requires different standards of grammar. For example, in more relaxed writing, jargon and clichés are okay, whereas technical writing has longer and more complex sentences.

For these different kettles of fish, Grammatik lets you choose from several different writing styles and levels of formality. And, if you're feeling spunky enough, you can even create your own custom styles. The next few sections tell you everything you need to know.

Selecting a Different Style

To select a different style, pull down the Options menu and select the **Writing Style** command. You'll see the Writing Style dialog box, shown below.

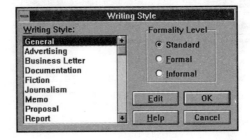

Use the Writing Style screen to choose a different writing style.

Before choosing a style, you might want to review its individual grammar settings. To do this, highlight the style you want in the **Writing Style** list and then select the Edit button. The Writing Style Settings dialog box that appears shows you all of Grammatik's rule classes and which ones have been selected for the current style. Grammatik divides the rule classes into three sections: **Style**, **Grammar**, and **Mechanical**. Selecting any of these option buttons displays the different rule classes associated with each one. When you're done, select **Cancel** to return to the Writing Style dialog box. (You select **OK** only when you want to create a custom writing style. See "Creating a Custom Style," on the next page.)

To choose a different style, just highlight it in the **Writing Style** list and then select **OK**.

Changing the Formality Level

The level of *formality* is a measure of how exacting Grammatik is when it checks your documents. The Informal level is the most easygoing (it'll accept contractions, such as *it'll*, for example), while the Formal level won't let you get away with too much.

In version 5.2, select Writing Style from the Preferences menu. To see the settings for a particular style, highlight it and select the View Style Settings button.

To change the formality level, select the Option menu's Writing Style command and, in the Writing Style dialog box, select either Standard, Informal, or Formal. Select **OK** to return to Grammatik.

Creating a Custom Style

Once you've used Grammatik for a while, you may notice that certain types of ignorable errors keep cropping up. For example, Grammatik may complain about sentences being too long, or numbers that should be spelled out (for example, using "two" instead of "2"). Believe me, it doesn't take long before these things get awfully annoying. The remedy isn't to chuck Grammatik out the window, but to create your own styles that don't check for these errors.

Here are the steps to follow to create your own custom style:

1. Pull down the Options menu and select the Writing Style command to display the Writing Style dialog box.

In version 5.2, select the Customize button in the Writing Style screen.

2. If an existing style is close to the one you want to create, highlight it in the Writing Style list. Then select the Edit button to display the Writing Style Settings dialog box.

By the Way . . .

Grammatik lets you create up to three custom styles (named Custom 1, Custom 2, and Custom 3). The Writing Style Settings dialog box shows you the name your custom style will use in the upper right corner (for example, **Save To Style: Custom 1**).

3. Go through the rules on the screen, activating those you want to use, and deactivating those you want to ignore. Make sure you cover all three categories (Style, Grammar, and Mechanical).

4. When you're done, select **OK**. Grammatik adds the new style to the **Writing Style** list.

5. Select **OK** to return to Grammatik and use your custom style.

Put It to Work

WordPerfect for Windows' Speller checks spelling, doubled words, and unusual capitalizations anyway (see Chapter 20), so you can speed up Grammatik by creating a custom style that doesn't use these checks. You'll find each of these rules on the Mechanical Rules screen.

The Least You Need to Know

This chapter showed you the ins and outs of using Grammatik, WordPerfect for Windows 6's new grammar-checking program. Here's a recap:

- ☞ To start Grammatik, select **G**rammatik from the **T**ools menu.

- ☞ When Grammatik flags a possible error, you can edit the document text directly, turn off the Rule Class check box, or use the buttons in the Grammatik window to tell the program what to do next.

- ☞ Grammatik can allow for different writing styles. To work with a different style, select the **W**riting Style command from the **O**ptions menu and choose the style you want from the dialog box that appears.

- ☞ The Writing Style dialog box also lets you change the level of formality. Just select an option from the Formality Level group.

This page unintentionally left blank.

Chapter 22
Working with Graphics

In This Chapter

- Sprucing up your documents with clip art
- Creating fancy boxes for your text
- Drawing lines
- Playing with the new TextArt feature
- More fun timewasting tools that just about guarantee you'll never get your work done

Television commercials assure us nowadays that "image is everything." And since they couldn't put it on TV if it wasn't true (!), we need to think about what kind of image our documents present to the outside world. You've seen in earlier chapters how a few fonts and other formatting options can do wonders for drab, lifeless text. But *anybody* can do that kind of stuff. To make your documents really stand out from the crowd, you need to go graphical with clip-art figures, lines, and boxes. Happily, WordPerfect for Windows has the tools that not only get the job done, but make the whole thing a snap. This chapter gives you the graphics nitty-gritty.

Working with Graphics Boxes

Most WordPerfect for Windows graphics appear inside *graphics boxes*. These boxes are like islands floating in the sea of your document because the regular text flows around them. But unlike real islands, graphics boxes can be moved and sized and you can apply a fistful of formatting options to them.

What can you put inside a graphics box? Well, all kinds of things, really, but the most common are clip-art images and text (which I'll look at in this chapter), and drawings (which I'll cover in Chapter 23).

Adding a Clip-Art Figure to a Document

Chapter 23, "Drawing with WordPerfect Draw," shows you how to create your own drawings and add them to a document. If you have neither the time, inclination, nor talent for these artistic endeavors, not to worry. WordPerfect for Windows comes with its own *clip-art* collection. Clip art is professional-quality artwork that you can incorporate into your documents free of charge. You get over one hundred images of everything from an accordion to a zipper. But the real fun begins after you've added the graphic because you can then move it around, change its size, rotate it, add a caption, you name it.

If you want to see the image before inserting it, remember you can select the View button to see a preview of the highlighted file.

Adding a clip-art figure is as easy as opening a file. The first thing you should do is position the insertion point where you want the image to appear in the document. Then pull down the Graphics menu and select Figure. WordPerfect for Windows displays the Insert Image dialog box, which is similar to the other directory dialogs you've seen (such as Open File and Save As). In this case, WordPerfect for Windows displays the GRAPHICS subdirectory that contains the clip-art files. Highlight the file you want to open from the Filename list and then select **OK** or press **Enter**.

WordPerfect for Windows creates a graphics box (or, more specifically in this case, a *figure box*), inserts the image inside the box, and displays the Graphics Box feature bar (see the figure, below).

Once you have your image in the document, you can move it around, change its size, add a caption, and more. I'll show you how to do these things later in this section. For now, you can return to the document by clicking outside of the graphics box.

> ## By the Way . . .
>
> Many of the clip-art files (for example, APPROVED.WPG and ASAP.WPG) contain only a couple of words and no real artwork at all. What gives? These files are for creating *watermarks*—translucent images or bits of text that print "underneath" the existing text on a page. If you'd like to try this out, select the **Watermark** command from the Layout menu, and then select **C**reate from the Watermark dialog box. In the Watermark feature bar that appears, select **F**igure and then insert one of the graphics files.

Adding a Text Box

Throughout this book I've placed various notes, tips, and cautions in separate sections like this:

> ## By the Way . . .
>
> Placing text in its own box like this is a great way to highlight important material and catch the reader's attention.

You can do the same thing in your WordPerfect for Windows documents by creating a text box. Again, position the insertion point where you want the box to appear and then select Text from the Graphics menu. WordPerfect displays a box with its own insertion point as well as the Graphics Box feature bar. Now enter your text just as you would in the typing area (see the following page). When you're done, you can return to the document by clicking outside of the text box.

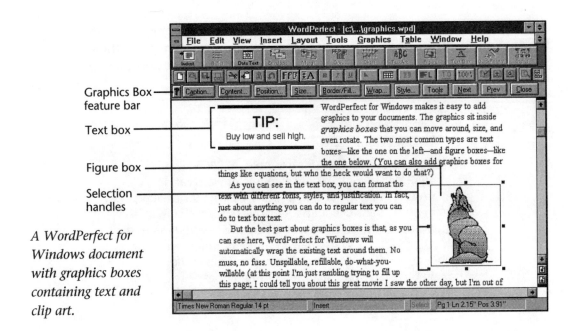

Graphics Box feature bar

Text box

Figure box

Selection handles

A WordPerfect for Windows document with graphics boxes containing text and clip art.

Selecting a Graphics Box

If you need to make changes to a graphics box, you have to select it first. There are four methods you can use:

☞ Click on the graphics box.

☞ Click on **Next** (or press **Alt+Shift+N**) or **Prev** (**Alt+Shift+R**) from the feature bar to cycle through the graphic boxes in order.

☞ If your document has only one graphics box, select the Edit Box command from the Graphics menu, or press **Shift+F11**.

☞ If your document has multiple graphics boxes and you don't feel like cycling through them, things get a little stickier. First select Edit Box from the Graphics menu to display the Box Find dialog box. Now you have two choices: select Document Box Number and enter the number of the graphics box (WordPerfect for Windows numbers the boxes according to their position in the document); or select the type of box from the Counters list, activate the Counter Number option, and then enter the number of the type of box you selected. Select **OK** to get the heck out of there.

Every graphics box has a border that defines its boundaries. When you select a box, WordPerfect for Windows displays black *selection handles* around the frame. (Take a look at the figure box in the picture shown earlier to see an example of these selection handles.)

Adding a Caption to a Graphics Box

Captions are an easy way to add explanatory text to a figure box or other graphic. Here are the steps to follow:

1. Select the graphics box you want to work with.

2. Click on Caption (or press **Alt+Shift+A**) in the feature bar. WordPerfect for Windows displays the Box Caption dialog box.

3. Use the controls in the **Caption Position** group to change the position of the caption, if necessary.

4. Select the Edit button. WordPerfect for Windows returns you to the document, displays the default caption, and starts the Caption Editor.

5. Edit the caption and enter the text you want.

6. When you're done, click outside the graphics box or select Close from the File menu.

By the Way . . .

The commands discussed in this section and many of the following sections are also available in the QuickMenu for each graphics box. Just right-click on the box to see the QuickMenu list.

Editing the Contents of a Graphics Box

If you want to change the text inside a text box, or the figure inside a figure box, select the Content button from the feature bar (or press

Alt+Shift+O). This displays the Box Content dialog box. You have two options:

You can also edit text box text by simply double-clicking inside the box.

- For a figure box, use the browse button to the right of the Filename text box to select a different clip-art file.

- For a text box, select the Edit button. WordPerfect for Windows returns you to the document and activates the Text Box Editor. Make your changes and then either click outside the box or select Close from the File menu.

Moving a Graphics Box

When you add a graphics box to a document, its position isn't set in stone, so you can move it anywhere you like. There are two methods you can use:

- With your mouse, position the mouse pointer inside the box you want to move and then drag the box to its new location. (As you're dragging, the mouse pointer changes to a four-sided arrow and you'll see a dotted outline around the box. This is perfectly normal behavior.)

OR

- Click on Position in the feature bar (or press **Alt+Shift+P**) to display the Box Position dialog box. Use the controls in the **Position Box** group to set the new position for the box. When you're done, select **OK**.

Sizing a Graphics Box

If a graphics box doesn't have the dimensions you want, it's no problem changing the size. Again, you can use either of two methods:

- With your mouse, select the box you want to size and then drag one of the selection handles until the box is the size and shape you want. Which selection handle should you use? Well, if you want to change the size horizontally or vertically, use the appropriate handle on the middle of a side. To change the size in two directions at once, use the appropriate corner handle.

OR

☞ Click on Size in the feature bar (or press **Alt+Shift+S**) to open the Box Size dialog box. Use **Box Size** group controls to set the width and height and then select **OK**.

Setting the Border and Fill Styles for a Graphics Box

As I mentioned earlier, every graphics box has a border surrounding it. A figure box displays its entire border, but text boxes only show the top and bottom. If you'd like something with a little more pizzazz, WordPerfect for Windows comes with over two dozen different border styles.

But wait, there's more. You can also change something called the *fill style*. The fill style is the background on which the contents of the box are displayed. The default is plain white, but there are all kinds of weird and wonderful patterns you can use. Here are some example boxes with various borders and fill styles.

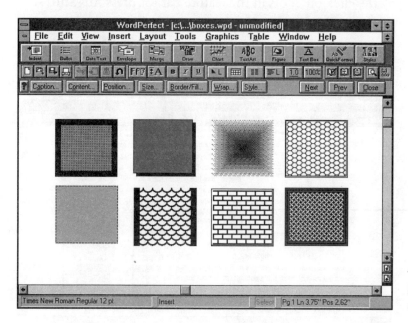

A few of WordPerfect for Windows' border and fill styles.

To change the border and fill styles, select the box you want to work with and then click on Border/Fill in the feature bar (or press **Alt+Shift+B**). In the Box Border/Fill Styles dialog box, use the Border Style and Fill Style options to select the styles you want. Select **OK** when you're done.

Wrapping Text Around a Graphics Box

One of the things that makes graphics boxes so easy to use is that WordPerfect for Windows automatically wraps the regular document text around the box. And moving or sizing the box is no problem because the text adjusts along with the box.

By default, WordPerfect for Windows wraps text around the box border and wraps on the side of the object that has the largest amount of white space. To change these defaults, select **Wrap** from the feature bar (or press **Alt+Shift+W**) and then select your options from the Wrap Text dialog box.

Working with the Image Tools Palette

WordPerfect for Windows also includes a set of tools for working with the images inside figure boxes. The Image Tools Palette is a set of icons that controls image attributes, such as rotation, scaling, colors, and more. To display the palette, click on Tools in the feature bar (or press **Alt+Shift+L**). The palette appears next to the image, as you can see below.

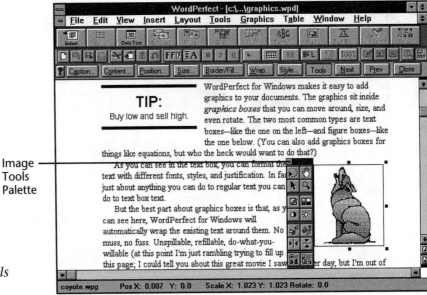

The Image Tools Palette.

Here's a summary of the available tools:

Rotate	Rotates the image. When selected, rotation handles appear around the image and you drag a handle to perform the rotation. The **Rotate** info in the status bar tells you the degrees of rotation.
Move	Moves the image within the box (not to be confused with moving the *entire* box, which we discussed earlier). When selected, the mouse pointer changes to a hand when you place it over the image. Drag the image to move it. The **Pos** X and **Y** info on the status bar tells you the current position.
Pointer	Resets the mouse pointer to its default behavior.
Scale	Scales the image. Selecting this tool displays three more: the magnifying glass scales a selected area by dragging; the double arrows scale the entire image using scroll bars; the **1:1** tool resets the image. The **Scale** X and **Y** Status Bar info tracks the current scale.
Complement	Changes the image colors to their complementary values (red changes to green, blue changes to yellow, etc.).
Black & White	Displays the image in black and white.
Contrast	Sets the contrast between the light and dark areas of the image. Select this tool and then choose a contrast level from the examples provided.
Brightness	Sets the brightness (or the *saturation*) of the colors in the image. Select this tool and then choose a brightness level from the example box.
Reset	Resets the image attributes to their original values.
Fill Attributes	Controls the colors inside the image. You can choose the normal colors, no colors, or white only.

Mirror Vertical	Flips the image along its vertical axis.
Mirror Horizontal	Flips the image along its horizontal axis.
Image Edit	Starts WordPerfect Draw to let you edit the image (see Chapter 23 to learn how to use WordPerfect Draw).
Image Settings	Displays the Image Settings dialog box to let you set values for most of the preceding tools.

To close the Image Tools Palette, double-click on the bar in the upper left corner of the Palette.

Deleting a Graphics Box

To delete a graphics box you no longer need, select it and then run the Cut command from the Edit menu or else press **Delete**.

Working with Lines

A simple line across a document is a great way to separate different sections of your text. WordPerfect for Windows lets you add either horizontal or vertical lines, and you can customize each line by setting different styles, colors, and lengths.

Adding a Line

To add a line to a document, position the insertion point where you want the line to appear, pull down the Graphics menu, and then select either Horizontal Line (or press **Ctrl+F11**) or Vertical Line (or press **Ctrl+Shift+F11**). WordPerfect for Windows inserts the new line at the insertion point.

Selecting a Line

To select a line, simply click on it with your mouse. (Unlike with graphic boxes, WordPerfect for Windows has no way of selecting a line from the keyboard.) When you select a line, you'll see the usual selection handles surrounding it.

Moving a Line

To move a line, you can use either of the following methods:

☞ Drag the line to its new location.

OR

☞ Select the line and then select the Edit Line command from the Graphics menu. In the Edit Graphics Line dialog box, use the Horizontal and Vertical controls to set the new position for the line. When you're done, select **OK**.

Sizing a Line

You can size a line either lengthwise (to make it longer or shorter) or widthwise (to make it thicker or thinner). You can use either of the following techniques:

☞ Select the line you want to size and then drag one of the selection handles until the line is the size and shape you want.

OR

☞ Select the line and then select the Graphics menu's Edit Line command. In the Edit Graphics Line dialog box, use the Length and Thickness controls to change the size and then select **OK**.

Setting the Line Style and Color

As with graphics boxes, WordPerfect for Windows offers a number of styles and colors for your graphics lines. To check them out, select Edit Line from the Graphics menu to display the Edit Graphics Line dialog box. The Line Style controls give you over 30 different styles to choose from. Some of the styles come with a preset color. If you'd like to use a different color, select one from the Line Color control.

Deleting a Line

To delete a line you no longer need, select it and then run the Edit menu's Cut command or else press **Delete**.

Playing with TextArt

One of the most addictive of WordPerfect for Windows 6's new features has got to be TextArt. This little utility can take plain, old text and bend it in all sorts of bizarre ways. You can also rotate the text, add shadows, place borders around each letter, and change the text colors and patterns. It's a lot of fun and, hey, it sure beats workin'.

Starting TextArt

To crank up TextArt, just select the TextArt command from the Graphics menu. In a few seconds you'll see the TextArt screen, as shown below.

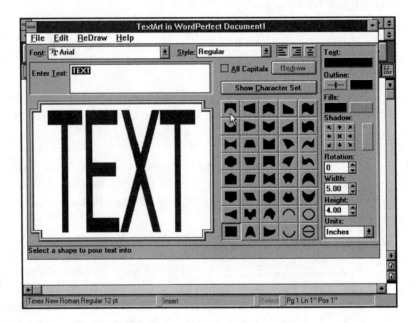

The TextArt screen is chock-full of fun font effects.

Using TextArt

TextArt is actually a separate program, so it comes complete with its own menu bar and status line (see the figure). To work with TextArt, you first type in the text you want to work with in the Enter Text box. You can enter up to 58 characters on up to three separate lines (press **Enter** to create a new line). You then modify the text using TextArt's numerous options, and the changes appear in the Image area. When you're done, you update the WordPerfect for Windows document, and TextArt inserts a graphics box containing the TextArt text.

Here's a quick review of the TextArt options:

By the Way . . .
To get a hint about what each TextArt option does, place the mouse pointer over the option and read the text that appears in the status line.

Font	Selects the typeface for the text.
Style	Selects the type style (regular, bold, italic, etc.).
Alignment	If you have multiple lines of text, these options control the alignment within the TextArt box.
All Capitals	Displays the text in uppercase only.

By the Way . . .
If you plan to use shapes to bend your text (see below), you'll find the resulting graphic looks better if the text uses capital letters only.

Redraw	This button refreshes the image area to reflect your selected options. This button is only active if you select the Manual command from TextArt's **ReDraw** menu.

Show Character Set	Displays the full character set for the selected font at the bottom of the screen. You can double-click on any of these symbols to copy them into the Enter Text area.
Shapes	Select one of these buttons and TextArt bends the text to fit the shape. Select the rectangle in the lower left corner to revert the text back to its normal shape.
Text	Sets the color of the text. Selecting this option displays a palette of 16 colors and 16 shades of gray.
Outline	These two buttons control the outline around characters. The left button sets the thickness of the outline. (The line with the X through it means no outline, and the line with two arrows means a hairline outline.) The button on the left sets the outline color.
Fills	These two buttons control the text fill pattern and background color. (The foreground color is determined by the Text option, above.)
Shadow	These two buttons control the text shadow. The 9 arrows set the direction of the shadow (the X in the middle removes the shadow). Repeatedly clicking an arrow moves the shadow further from the text. The button on the right controls the color of the shadow.
Rotation	Rotates the text. Enter the number of degrees to rotate the image, or use the spinner to adjust the rotation 45 degrees at a time.
Width	Adjusts the width of the image. The numbers you use depend on the units you select (see below). Here are the limits for each unit:

Unit	Minimum	Maximum
Inches	0.5	8
Picas	3	48
Points	36	576
Centimeters	1.27	20.32

Height	Adjusts the height of the image. Again, the numbers you use depend on the units. The maximums and minimums are the same as those listed for Width.
Units	The measurements units to use for the width and height.

Saving Your Work

While tinkering with your text, it's a good idea to save your work every so often. You have two ways to do this:

- ☛ To add the graphic to the current WordPerfect for Windows document, select Update WordPerfect from the File menu.

- ☛ If you'd like to save the graphic in a separate file for later use, select the File menu's Save Copy As command. This displays a Save As dialog box (that works just like the one for WordPerfect for Windows).

If you haven't saved your work when you exit TextArt (by selecting the Exit & Return to WordPerfect command from the File menu), the program will ask "Update embedded object(s) in WordPerfect?" Select Yes to add the TextArt graphic to your document.

An "embedded object" is a graphic or file that was created in one program and now resides in another. (This is the "embedding" part of Object Linking and Embedding.) In this case, the graphic you created in TextArt now resides in (or, to use the vernacular, is *embedded* in) a WordPerfect for Windows document.

Working with the TextArt Graphics Box

When TextArt adds the graphic to your document, it places it in a graphics box just like the ones you saw earlier for figures and text. This means that you can use the same feature bar options to add a caption or move and size the text. If you want to use TextArt to make changes to the graphic, you just have to double-click on the box and TextArt will load automatically. (Alternatively, you can select the graphics box, and then run the Edit TextArt Object command from the Edit menu.)

The Least You Need to Know

This chapter took you through some of WordPerfect for Windows fun graphics tools. Here's what happened:

- ☞ You can insert graphics boxes anywhere in your document and WordPerfect for Windows will automatically wrap the existing text around the box.

- ☞ To include clip-art images in a document, select the **G**raphics menu's **F**igure command and then select a clip-art file from the Insert Image dialog box.

- ☞ To include a text box, select **T**ext from the **G**raphics menu.

- ☞ Use the Graphics Box Feature bar to change box attributes, such as captions, contents, position, and size.

- ☞ To add a line to your document, pull down the **G**raphics menu and select either **H**orizontal Line or **V**ertical Line.

- ☞ For a good graphics time, run the TextArt command and go crazy with the TextArt program's special effects.

Chapter 23
Drawing with WordPerfect Draw

In This Chapter

- Navigating the WordPerfect Draw window
- Drawing lines, boxes, circles, and other shapes
- Drawing freehand lines
- Editing your drawings

If you enjoyed finger painting when you were a kid, you'll get a kick out of WordPerfect Draw, the drawing program that comes free with WordPerfect for Windows. Oh sure, you can use it for practical stuff like logos, charts, and whatnot, but to my mind, WordPerfect Draw's real reason for being is sheer fun. Think about it: all you do is select a "tool" to work with and then just wiggle your mouse around the screen. Magically, you get all kinds of cool shapes and patterns. Throw in a few colors, and you have a recipe for hours of entertainment.

Starting WordPerfect Draw

To start WordPerfect Draw, select the Draw command from the Graphics menu. You'll see the WP Draw window shown on the following page.

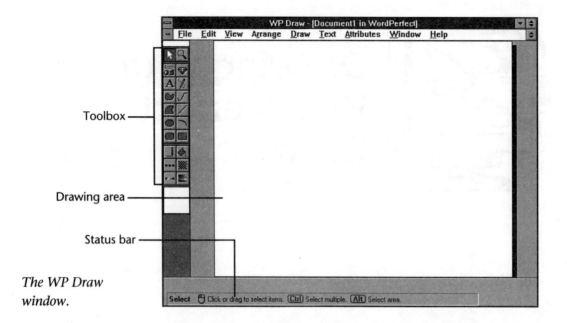

The WP Draw
window.

A Tour Around the WP Draw Window

WordPerfect Draw is a separate program, so it has its own menu bar
(thankfully, it works just like the one in WordPerfect for Windows). The
rest of this section gives you a rundown of the other parts of the WP Draw
screen.

The Title Bar

This section shows you the name of the program as well as the name of
the current WordPerfect for Windows document. It will also show you
hints when you highlight a menu bar command or position the mouse
pointer over a Toolbox tool.

The Toolbox

This area contains the various "tools" that you use to create or work with
your drawings. (The Toolbox is only available to mouse users. Keyboard
types use the menu bar commands.) The Toolbox is divided into three
sections: selection tools, drawing tools, and attribute tools.

The selection tools let you select drawing elements for copying and moving and change the view of the drawing. Table 23.1 gives you the details.

Table 23.1   The Toolbox Selection Tools

Tool	Description
	Selects portions of the drawing for moving, copying, or deleting.
	Lets you zoom in on a piece of the drawing for detail work.

The drawing tools are what you use to draw your lines and shapes. Table 23.2 takes you through each tool.

Table 23.2   The Toolbox Drawing Tools

Tool	Description
	Loads WordPerfect Draw's Chart Editor to let you create fancy bar charts, pie charts, and more.
	Inserts a graphic image in the drawing.
	Inserts text in the drawing.
	Draws a freehand line.
	Draws a curved shape.
	Draws a curve.
	Draws a shape with angular corners.
	Draws a line.

continues

Table 23.2   Continued

Tool	Description
	Draws an ellipse or circle.
	Draws an arc.
	Draws a rectangle or square with rounded corners.
	Draws a rectangle or square.

The attributes tools control things like the color and line style of each shape you draw. Table 23.3 gives you the lowdown on each tool.

Table 23.3   The Toolbox Attributes Tools

Tool	Description
	Toggles the object's outline on or off.
	For closed objects, such as a circle or rectangle, toggles the interior pattern on or off.
	Displays a box of line styles for the object's outline. You just click on the thickness and pattern you want to use.
	Displays a box of patterns for the object's interior. Click on the pattern you want.
	Displays the WordPerfect Draw color palette so you can select the color of the object's outline.
	Displays the color palette so you can select the color of the interior of the object.

The Drawing Area

This is the large, blank expanse that takes up most of the WP Draw window. It's where you draw and paint your objects!

The Status Bar

When you select a tool, this area lets you know what mouse and keyboard actions you can use with the tool.

Drawing with WordPerfect Draw

The best way to approach WordPerfect Draw is simply to have fun fooling around with the various tools and colors. However, there *is* a basic method you can use for each tool:

1. Select a drawing tool from the Toolbox (or from the Draw menu).

2. Use the attribute tools (or the At-tributes menu) to select tool at-tributes, such as the color and line style.

3. Move the pointer into the drawing area and draw the shape you want.

If you make a mess during the drawing, you can start again by simply pressing the **Escape** key *before* you finish drawing the shape. If you've already finished the shape, you can still get rid of it by selecting **Undo** from the **Edit** menu.

Drawing Ellipses, Arcs, and Rectangles

You can use the Ellipse, Elliptical Arc, Rounded Rectangle, and Rectangle tools to create most of the basic building blocks for your drawing. To use them, first select the appropriate tool and then set up the attributes (if any) you want to use. Move the mouse pointer into the drawing area and position it where you want the shape to start. The pointer, you'll notice, changes to a cross. Now drag the pointer until the object is the size and shape you want and then release the mouse button.

To draw a perfect circle, circular arc, or square, hold down the **Shift** key while dragging the mouse. To draw an ellipse or rectangle from its center (instead of an edge), hold down **Alt** while dragging. For an arc, holding down **Alt** inverts the arc.

Put It to Work

WordPerfect Draw's rectangles are perfect for creating company organization charts. You can use the Line tool (described in the next section) to join the boxes, and the Text tool (described later on) to add people's names and job titles.

Drawing Curves and Lines

The following steps show you how to use the Closed Curve, Curve, Polygon, and Line tools:

1. Select the tool and attributes you want to use.

2. Position the pointer where you want the object to start. Then press and hold down the left mouse button.

3. Drag the mouse until the first line is the length you want and then release the button.

4. Drag the mouse again either to draw a second line (in the case of the Polygon and Line tools) or to curve the line (for the Closed Curve and Curve tools). Release the button when you're done.

5. If you want to add more line or curves, repeat step 4.

6. When you're done, double-click to finish the object.

If you hold down the **Shift** key while dragging the mouse, WordPerfect Draw will limit the angles of your lines and curves. You'll only be able to draw them straight up and down, left or right, or at 45-degree angles.

Drawing Freehand Lines

As you've seen, WordPerfect Draw makes it easy to draw lines, circles, and polygons. Too easy, some would say. For a real challenge, try using the Freehand tool to draw lines that follow the mouse pointer. Begin by selecting the Freehand tool and, if you like, a line style and line color. Now position the mouse pointer where you want to start drawing (it changes, as usual, to a cross) and then drag the mouse. As you drag, a line follows your every move.

Adding Text to a Drawing

WordPerfect Draw is mostly for your right brain, but if your left brain wants to get in on the act, you can use the Text tool to add text to a drawing. Here's what you do:

1. Select the **Text** tool from the Toolbox.

2. Move the pointer into the drawing area and position it where you want the text to appear.

3. Drag the mouse to create a box for the text. Release the button when the box is the size and shape you want.

4. Use the commands on the **Text** menu (**F**ont, **B**old, etc.) to define the format you want to use for the text.

5. Enter your text in the box. When you're done, click outside the box to add the text to the drawing.

Adding a Figure to a Drawing

One of the easiest ways to get the drawing you want is to start with one of WordPerfect for Windows' clip-art files and modify it to suit your needs. To try this out, select the **Figure** tool, move the pointer into the drawing area, and then drag the mouse to create a box for the figure. When you release the button, WordPerfect Draw displays the Retrieve Figure dialog box. Highlight the file you want to use (you may have to change to the GRAPHICS subdirectory), and then select the **Retrieve** button. WordPerfect Draw inserts the file into the box.

Working with Objects

Once you've added an object or two to your drawing, you may need to make adjustments to the size, position, or attributes of an object. This section shows you how to do this.

Selecting an Object

You need to select an object before you can work with it. WordPerfect Draw gives you four different methods:

☛ To select a single object, click on the **Select** tool and then click on the object you want. WordPerfect Draw surrounds the object with *selection handles*, as shown below.

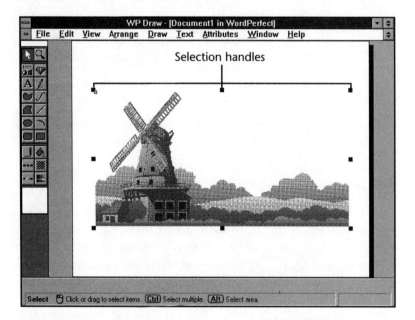

When you select an object, WordPerfect Draw surrounds it with selection handles.

☛ To select multiple objects, click on the **Select** tool and then hold down **Ctrl** as you click on each object.

☛ To select all the objects in a specific area of the drawing, click on the **Select** tool, move the pointer into the drawing area, and then drag the mouse to create a box. WordPerfect Draw selects every object that is completely inside the box.

☛ To select every object in the drawing, run the Edit menu's Select command and then choose All from the cascade menu. In the Chart Editor, Select All is your only option—you can't select one element.

> ## By the Way . . .
> Once you've selected an object, you can easily change its attributes. Just click on the appropriate attribute tool and select the new setting.

Moving an Object

To get your drawing just right, you may need to move some of the objects around. This is no sweat: click on the **Select** tool and position the pointer inside the object. Then just drag the mouse to move the object to its new home. To help out, WordPerfect Draw displays an outline of the object as you move it.

> To make a copy of an object, hold down **Ctrl** while dragging the mouse.

Sizing an Object

Until you get used to the WordPerfect Draw tools, one of the hardest things to do is get the right size for your objects. Fortunately, changing the size of a shape is easy. Just select the object you want to size and then drag one of the selection handles. Here are some things to keep in mind when sizing:

☛ To change the width, drag the left or right side handles away from the object (to make it fatter) or inside the object (to make it skinnier).

☛ To change the height of an object, drag the top or bottom handles away from the object (to make it taller) or inside the object (to make it shorter).

☛ To change both the width and height at the same time, drag the corner handles.

☛ To change two sides (either the left and right or the top and bottom) at once, hold down **Alt** while dragging a handle.

☛ To leave the original object intact, hold down **Ctrl** while dragging the handles.

Deleting an Object

While you're getting used to WordPerfect Draw, you'll likely end up with a few failed experiments that you don't want in your finished drawing. To remove these rogue elements, select them and then either select Cut from the Edit menu or press **Delete**. If the drawing is a complete disaster and you want to start with a fresh slate, select the File menu's Clear command.

Adding a Drawing to Your Document

The purpose of WordPerfect Draw, let us not forget, is to add a drawing to the current WordPerfect for Windows document. You have two ways to do this:

- ☞ To add the drawing to the document without exiting WordPerfect Draw, select Update *document* from the File menu (where *document* is the name of the current document).

- ☞ To add the drawing when you exit WordPerfect Draw, select the File menu's Exit and Return to *document* command (again, *document* will be the name of the current WordPerfect for Windows file). This displays the WP Draw dialog box, which asks if you want to save your changes. Select Yes to add the drawing to your document.

When WordPerfect Draw adds the drawing to your document, it places it in a *graphics box*. To learn how to work with graphics boxes, see Chapter 22, "Working with Graphics." If you want to use WordPerfect Draw to make changes to the drawing, you just have to double-click on the box and WordPerfect Draw will load automatically. (You can also select the graphics box, and then run the Edit WP Graphic 2.1 Object command from the Edit menu.)

Adding a Chart to a Drawing

If you plan to include numbers in your document (such as last year's sales figures or next year's budget), you can spice things up by displaying the numbers in a chart. WordPerfect Draw comes with a Chart Editor that lets you enter your numbers in a spreadsheet-like table. Chart Editor then creates the chart automatically.

If you feel like giving it a go, select the **Chart** tool, move the pointer into the drawing area, and then drag the mouse to create a box for the chart. When you release the button, WordPerfect Draw displays the Create Chart dialog box. Select the kind of chart you want and then select **OK**. (If you're not sure what the various chart types mean, select Gallery to display the Chart Gallery dialog box. Click on one of the eight chart types and then select Chart Styles. Click on a style and then select the **Retrieve** button.) The next thing you'll see is the Chart Editor screen, shown below.

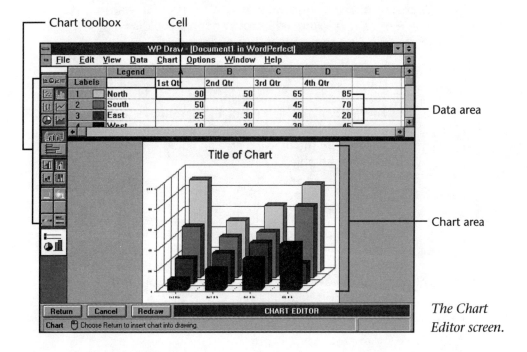

The Chart Editor screen.

Besides a new menu bar for the Chart Editor commands, this screen also displays the following elements:

Toolbox This toolbox is different from the normal WordPerfect Draw toolbox. The new buttons let you select the chart type and chart style you want to use.

Data area This area displays a table where you can enter the data for the chart. WordPerfect Draw displays some sample data, but feel free to make whatever changes you need. If you've never used a spreadsheet before, each of the white rectangles in the data area is called a *cell*. You click on a cell and then just type in what you want. When you make changes, click on the **Redraw** button to update the chart.

Chart area   This area shows you what your chart will look like. Use the commands in the Options menu to format the chart the way you want it.

When you've finished, click on **Return** to add the chart to the drawing.

The Least You Need to Know

This chapter showed you how to have all sorts of fun with WordPerfect Draw, WordPerfect for Windows' cool drawing program. Here's a summary of the important stuff:

- ☞ To load WordPerfect Draw, select **Draw** from the Graphics menu.

- ☞ To start drawing, first select a tool from the Toolbox and any attributes you need. Then move the pointer into the drawing area and drag the mouse to create an object.

- ☞ Use the Select tool to select pieces of your drawing for moving, sizing, or deleting.

- ☞ To add a drawing to the current WordPerfect for Windows document, pull down the File menu and select either **Update** *document* or Exit and Return to *document* (where *document* is the name of the current document).

Speak Like a Geek Glossary

active window   The window you're currently slaving away in. You can tell a window is active if it has the blinking *insertion point*, or if its title bar is a darker color than the other windows' title bars.

alphanumeric keypad   The keyboard area that contains the letters, numbers (the ones across the top row, not the ones on the *numeric keypad*), and punctuation symbols.

ASCII text file   A file that uses only the American Standard Code for Information Interchange character set (which is just techno-lingo for the characters you see on your keyboard).

block   A selection of text in a document.

boilerplate   Text that you reuse over and over. It's the word processing equivalent of the old maxim, "Don't reinvent the wheel."

boot   Computer geeks won't tell you to start your computer; they'll tell you to *boot* it. This doesn't mean you should punt your monitor across the room. The term *booting* comes from the phrase "pulling oneself up by one's own bootstraps," which just means that your computer can load everything it needs to operate properly without any help from the likes of you and me.

byte   Computerese for a single character of information. So for example, the phrase "This phrase is 28 bytes long" is, yes, 28 bytes long. (You count the spaces too—but not the quotation marks.)

cascade   A cool way of arranging windows so that they overlap each other while still letting you see the top of each window.

cascade menu   A menu that appears when you select certain *pull-down menu* commands.

character formatting   Changing the attributes of individual characters by adding things such as bolding or italics, or by using different fonts.

character set   A collection of related characters.

check box   A square-shaped switch that toggles a *dialog box* option on or off. The option is toggled on when an "X" appears in the box.

click   To quickly press and release the left mouse button.

clipboard   An area that holds data temporarily during cut-and-paste operations.

command button   A rectangular doohickey (usually found in *dialog boxes*) that, when chosen, runs whatever command is spelled out on its label.

commands   The options you see in a *pull-down menu*. You use these commands to tell WordPerfect for Windows what you want it to do next.

delay   The amount of time it takes for a second character to appear when you press and hold down a key.

dialog boxes   Ubiquitous windows that pop up on the screen to ask you for information, or to seek confirmation of an action you requested (or sometimes just to say "Hi").

directory   A storage location on your hard disk for keeping related files together. If your hard disk is like a house, a directory is like a room inside the house. See also *subdirectory*.

disk   See *floppy disk*.

double-click   To quickly press and release the left mouse button *twice* in succession.

drag   To press and *hold down* the left mouse button and then move the mouse.

drop-down list   A *dialog box* control that normally shows only a single item but, when selected, displays a list of options.

edit box   A screen area you use to type in text information, such as a description or a file name.

endnote   A section of text placed at the end of a document that usually contains asides or comments that embellish something in the regular document text. See also *footnote*.

extension   The three-character ending to a DOS file name. The extension is separated from the main name by a period.

file   An organized unit of information inside your computer. If you think of your hard disk as a house, files can be either servants (your programs) or things (data used by you or by a program).

floppy disk   A portable storage medium that consists of a flexible disk protected by a plastic case. Floppy disks are available in a variety of sizes and capacities.

font   A distinctive graphic design of letters, numbers, and other symbols.

footer   A section of text that appears at the bottom margin of each page in a document. See also *header*.

footnote   A section of text placed at the bottom of a page. It usually contains asides or comments that embellish something in the regular document text. See also *endnote*.

formatting   The process of setting up a disk so it can read and write information. Not to be confused with *character formatting*.

frame   A border that surrounds a *window* and lets you *maximize, minimize,* move, and size the window.

fritterware   Any software that causes you to fritter away time fiddling with its various bells and whistles.

function keys   The keys located either to the left of the *numeric keypad*, or across the top of the keyboard. There are usually 10 function keys (although some keyboards have 12), and they're labeled F1, F2, and so on. In WordPerfect for Windows, you use these keys either by themselves or as part of key combinations.

hard page break   A *page break* that you insert yourself. Text always breaks at this point, regardless of the margin sizes.

header   A section of text that appears at the top margin of each page in a document. See also *footer*.

hyphenation   The process in which WordPerfect for Windows splits larger words in two at the end of a line and inserts a hyphen. This can help improve the spacing in your paragraphs.

insertion point   The vertical bar (it's horizontal in *text mode*) you see inside WordPerfect for Windows' typing area; it tells you where the next character you type will appear.

insertion point control keys   The keys (which you'll find on a separate keypad, or mixed in with the *numeric keypad*) that you use to navigate a document.

kilobyte   1,024 *bytes*. Usually abbreviated as just *K*.

landscape orientation   When the lines on a page run across the long side of the page. See also *portrait orientation*.

margins   The empty spaces that surround your text on the page. WordPerfect for Windows' standard margins are one inch high on the top and bottom edges of the page, and one inch wide on the left and right edges.

maximize   To increase the size of a window to its largest extent. See also *minimize*.

megabyte   1,024 *kilobytes* or 1,048,576 *bytes*. The cognoscenti write this as *M* or *MB* and pronounce it *meg*.

menu bar   The horizontal bar just below the title bar in the WordPerfect for Windows screen. The menu bar contains the *pull-down menus.*

minimize   To reduce the size of a window to its smallest extent. See also *maximize.*

numeric keypad   A separate keypad for entering numbers on most keyboards. It actually serves two functions: when the Num Lock key is on, you can use it to enter numbers; if Num Lock is off, the keypad insertion point movement keys are enabled, and you can use them to navigate a document. Some keyboards (called extended keyboards) have a separate insertion point keypad so you can keep Num Lock on all the time.

option buttons   *Dialog box* options that appear as small circles in groups of two or more. Only one option from a group can be chosen.

orphan   A formatting error in which the first line in a paragraph appears by itself at the end of a page. See also *widow.*

page break   A line that appears across the screen, telling you where one page ends and the next one begins.

point   To move the mouse pointer so it rests on a specific screen location.

port   The connection you use to plug in the cable from a device such as a mouse or printer.

portrait orientation   When the lines run across the short side of a page. This is the standard way most pages are oriented. See also *landscape orientation.*

pull-down menus   Hidden menus that you open from WordPerfect for Windows' *menu bar* to access the program's commands and features.

RAM   Stands for Random Access Memory. The memory in your computer that DOS uses to run your programs.

repeat rate   After the initial *delay*, the rate at which characters appear when you press and hold down a key.

right-click   Press and release the right mouse button.

right ragged   Left-justified text. The right side of each line doesn't line up, so it looks ragged.

scroll bar   A bar that appears at the bottom or on the right of a window whenever the window is too small to display all of its contents.

scrolling   To move up or down through a document.

selection letter   The underlined letters in pull-down menu commands.

soft page break   A *page break* inserted automatically by WordPerfect for Windows. The position of the break depends on the margin sizes.

subdirectory   A *directory* within a directory.

type size   A measure of the height of a font. Type size is measured in *points*; there are 72 points in an inch.

Typeover mode   A WordPerfect for Windows mode where your typing replaces characters instead of being inserted between them. Use the Insert key to toggle between this mode and normal typing.

widow   A formatting error in which the last line in a paragraph appears by itself at the top of a page. See also *orphan*.

window   A screen area where WordPerfect for Windows displays your documents.

word processing   Using a computer to write, edit, format, and print documents. A high-end word processor, such as WordPerfect for Windows, also lets you add complicated features such as *footnotes* and indexes, and even has desktop publishing options that let you do true page layout stuff.

word wrap   A WordPerfect for Windows feature that starts a new line automatically as your typing reaches the end of the current line.

WYSIWYG   What-You-See-Is-What-You-Get. The ability to see on your computer screen what you end up getting from your printer. It's pronounced *wizzy wig*.

Index